How to Coach

How to Coach

Coaching yourself and your team to success

Jo Owen

PEARSON

Harlow, England • London • New York • Boston • San Francisco • Toronto • Sydney
Auckland • Singapore • Hong Kong • Tokyo • Seoul • Taipei • New Delhi
Cape Town • São Paulo • Mexico City • Madrid • Amsterdam • Munich • Paris • Milan

Pearson Education Limited
Edinburgh Gate
Harlow CM20 2JE
United Kingdom
Tel: +44 (0)1279 623623
Web: www.pearson.com/uk

First published 2013 (print and electronic)

© Jo Owen 2013 (print and electronic)

The right of Jo Owen to be identified as author of this work has been asserted by him in
accordance with the Copyright, Designs and Patents Act 1988.

Pearson Education is not responsible for the content of third-party internet sites.

ISBN: 978-0-273-78638-2 (print)
 978-0-273-79459-2 (PDF)
 978-0-273-79460-8 (ePub)

British Library Cataloguing-in-Publication Data
A catalogue record for the print edition is available from the British Library

Library of Congress Cataloging-in-Publication Data
A catalog record for the print edition is available from the Library of Congress

10 9 8 7 6 5 4 3 2 1
17 16 15 14 13

Typeset in 10pt Plantin Regular by 30
Print edition printed and bound in Great Britain by Ashford Colour Press Ltd,
Gosport, Hampshire

NOTE THAT ANY PAGE CROSS-REFERENCES REFER TO THE PRINT EDITION

Contents

Coaching skills and challenges index

Introduction

'War is too important to be left to the generals'[1]

Georges Clemenceau, French Prime Minister
during World War One

Coaching is too important to be left to coaches. Coaching is something all managers must master, if we want to improve ourselves and our teams.

It was not always this way. In the bad old days, bosses bossed and workers worked. Bosses had the brains and the workers had the hands. The world of command and control created clarity and certainty. It was a simple world, if not entirely comfortable for the workers.

And then things got complicated. The workers became educated. They could achieve more, but they demanded more. They were not just unreliable machines; they were human beings with hopes, fears and characters. Managers could no longer rely on just telling workers what to do. Managers had to work out how to get the best out of their teams.

We have been learning slowly how to make the most of teams: select the right team; give them the right tasks; train them; motivate them; manage performance. All these are important. But developing your team takes more than sending them off to a hotel for a couple of days of drinking, eating and training in the latest management theory. Training courses help with technical skills like accounting, but they are of little help with the difficult tasks of leading people and organisations.

I have asked thousands of executives in training courses how they have learned to lead. Think about how *you* have learned to lead, and see how you would answer the question I ask. Pick your two most important sources of learning about leadership from the following six possible sources of learning:

- books
- courses
- bosses (good and bad lessons)
- role models (inside or outside work)
- peers and colleagues
- personal experience.

If you have answered like most executives, you will have picked some combination of personal experience and observed experience of bosses, role models and colleagues. Books and training courses simply don't make the cut. That could be bad news for an author and a trainer.

In reality, this means that for many people the path to leadership is a random walk: we bump into good bosses and experience and we hit the motorway to success. We encounter poor experiences and bosses and we land up in a dead end. You cannot start a book at page 1 and finish at page 276 as the complete leader. But a good book will help you take some of the randomness out of the random walk of experience, and it will help you make sense of the nonsense you encounter from day to day.

As a manager, you have a vital role to play in developing your team. You may quietly be judging your team all the time; but they are also judging and learning from you all the time. You can let that learning happen by accident: you can hope that you are an effective role model for them. But if you really want your team to learn and grow it is not enough to be passive. You have to manage their growth actively: you have to be their coach.

the best learning … comes from discovering what works best

As a manager, the easy thing to do is totell team members what to do. It may be easy, but it does not help. The best learning does not come from being told what to do. It comes from discovering what works best.

The monkey puzzle

A team member has a problem and asks you for help. You understand the problem, sort it out and tell the team member what to do. You are pleased to have shown your capability, and the team member is pleased that the problem is solved.

Seeing that you are in a good mood, another team member decides to approach you with another nagging problem. Today, you are on a roll: you fix that problem as well and have another happy team member. Over the course of the day, each team member asks you for help and by the end of the day you have cemented your reputation as a decisive, insightful, helpful, problem-fixing manager. Congratulations. You have just failed.

Failed? When I did everything right? Are you nuts?

Let's call up the slow-motion action replay and see what really happened. The first team member had a troublesome monkey on her back. She gave it to you and left happy. And one by one all your team members unloaded their problem monkeys onto you. By the end of the day, you had a very happy team and a room full of manic monkeys to deal with. You had let your team delegate everything up to you.

Instead of taking the monkeys off their backs, you should have helped them learn how to deal with their monkeys themselves. And you might even have used the opportunity to give them one of your own monkeys as well. You would have helped them learn new skills and improve their collective performance, instead of learning to become dependent on you.

Helping team members discover how to deal with their monkeys takes time and effort. In the short term it is easier just to take the monkeys off their backs. In the long term, you and the team achieve far more if each team member knows how to deal with all the monkeys they are likely to face. Coaching is a long-term investment in the skills of each team member and the performance of the team as a whole.

The case for coaching is also growing because the nature of work is changing. Work is becoming more ambiguous and open ended. In the days when factory work dominated, productivity was a reasonably simple matter of quantity and quality: everyone knew when a bolt had been produced. You could count and measure bolts.

Office work is different. You never finish office work. A report could be three pages or 300 pages long, but there is always another fact or opinion you could gather. In practice, we have to rely on arbitrary constraints: we work to a deadline or to a budget. But budgets and deadlines are elastic to the extent that we simply work harder within these constraints to produce a quality output. So the search for quality within the unforgiving constraints of time and money means that we experience ever greater stress and effort.

The ambiguous nature of work matters. You can produce a manual and a training programme on how to produce burgers or bolts. These are 'know-what' skills that can be codified. But there is no manual for dealing with the ambiguity, uncertainty and conflicts of office life. These are the 'know-how' skills which are vital to survival and success. Most of us have to rely on the random walk of experience to find out what works and what does not in our very different worlds: what works here today may not work there tomorrow. The rules of the game are always changing.

This is where the good manager coach makes a difference. Your role is to help team members accelerate their journey of discovery. The emphasis is on discovery, not instruction. When we are told something, we may or may not believe it. When we discover it for ourselves, we absolutely believe it. We can observe this most clearly in toddlers: we can tell them not to touch a hot plate because it is dangerous. But curiosity is a powerful force. When the toddler finally touches the hot plate and discovers it *is* hot and dangerous, they have discovered a truth they will not forget. The discovered truth is valued more than the revealed truth: managers like to reveal the answer because that shows they are smart. A coach helps people discover the answer for themselves.

In the old world of command and control, managers did not need to coach. As we have already seen, coaching in today's world is essential for three reasons:

- Work is becoming more ambiguous and uncertain: training cannot deal with this.
- Employees are better educated and expect more: they do not expect to be subject to command and control.
- The way we learn essential 'know-how' skills is through discovery and experience, not through training.

The biggest argument against coaching is that it takes time which we do not have. It is easier and quicker to tell people the answer than to coach them. This is the same argument that is used by managers who do not delegate: it is quicker and easier to do it yourself. And that is true in the short term. But coaching is not a cost: it is an investment. By investing time now, you build capacity and capability for the future. Longer term, you build a

> coaching is not a cost: it is an investment

team which performs better and needs less support: you get a better result for less effort.

The second argument is that in a crisis you need to act fast. Again, this is true. When the house is burning down, you do not want to start a long coaching process to help your team discover their inner firefighter. But this is often a figleaf of an excuse. There are some managers who seem to live in a perpetual state of crisis: their house is always on fire and they are always heroically fighting the fires single-handed. It may be heroic, but it is not the sign of a good manager. They never have time to delegate, coach or support their team. A good manager should be in control, not in crisis.

As a manager, it is not enough to coach others. You have to be able to coach yourself. The random walk of experience can be a bruising way to learn. By learning to coach yourself, you accelerate your learning and you accelerate your career. You reduce your dependence on the vagaries of the assignment system and the whims of a boss who may or may not care or coach you well. And if you learn to coach yourself, you also become a better coach of your team members.

How to Coach is intended not for coaches, but for practising managers. The goal is to help you help your team and to help yourself. Over the years, coaching has become more professionalised, and less accessible to real managers. This is not good. There are countless different professional bodies which accredit coaches: each one claims to be the keeper of the true faith and is likely to condemn all the others as heretical upstarts. This is deeply unhelpful. It makes it seem as if coaching is the preserve of a professional elite, but it is unclear which elite is the 'right' elite.

Coaching is something which all managers should practise. *How to Coach* demystifies coaching and shows how you can coach your team to success. The coaching process is as simple as kicking a football. Anyone can do it, and the more you practise it the better you become.

coaching is something which all managers should practise

Part 1 of *How to Coach* lays out the coaching process. It is worth noting at this stage what coaching is and is not about. For a practising manager, coaching has four distinguishing characteristics:

- **Discovery, not instruction.** Managers tell the answer; coaches help people discover the answer. Discovery takes more time initially, but pays off in the long term with a better skilled and better performing team that takes more responsibility.

- **Journey, not transaction.** Coaching is not just a series of *ad hoc* discussions dealing with the latest crises. A good coaching relationship is a journey in which the coach manager helps each team member acquire some core capabilities over time. A good journey has a clear purpose and direction and is not a random walk.

- **Process and substance.** Some coaching is based on the principle 'answer every question with a question'. That is a good way of driving your team crazy. As a manager, you are expected to have insight and experience. The trick is to share your insight without telling people what to do. This trick lies at the heart of your success, which we explore in *How to Coach*.

- **Part of the job, not a separate activity.** Coaching is not separate from the day job: it is part of the day job. Making coaching part of the job requires a change of mindset for the manager and requires changing the psychological contract with his or her team. You have to move from pure hierarchy towards a partnership, even if hierarchy never disappears completely in any organisation.

Clearly, as a manager coach you cannot deal with every challenge your team member faces. In public your team members may support you and admire you. In private, they may think you are the problem, not the solution. You will be the last person to hear that. And if your team members need help in dealing with you, or in thinking through their careers, they will not talk to you. They will turn to outside help, and that might include a professional coach.

Having coached many executives over the last fifteen years, it is clear that there are some recurring themes in coaching conversations: dealing with conflict, managing the awkward squad, making decisions in uncertainty, making vital career decisions. These challenges are entirely predictable in any career, and there are fairly regular patterns of failure and success in dealing with these challenges.

Although the same questions come up time and again, the solutions are not the same each time. Each person and each situation is unique, so your solution is unique to you. But the patterns are familiar. To help yourself and your team, it pays to know these patterns.

Part 2 of *How to Coach* looks at the most common coaching questions in more detail. I do not give all the answers, because there are no standard answers. Instead, I share some simple frameworks for working through each challenge and arriving at a solution which works for you and for your team.

Part 1 shows you the principles of coaching and is worth reading straight through so that you understand the basics of coaching yourself and others. Part 2 is a resource for you to use when you face a challenge and are unsure of the best course of action. It will show you how the principles of Part 1 can be applied in practice. You can dip in and out of Part 2 as you need. Part 2 is effectively your personal coach. It deals with all the challenges you are most likely to face and shows how you can find solutions which work for you. You do not need to read the book from cover to cover.

How to Coach is not a grand theory. It is based on the real experience of real managers. It is about what works in practice, not what should work in theory. *How to Coach* does not attempt to reveal a truth which no one in management has ever thought about before: most such books are pretentious nonsense. *How to Coach* goes further. It shows how you can solve the messy problems that all

> *How to Coach* ... is about what works in practice, not what should work in theory

managers face day to day. It gives you the frameworks and toolkit for finding solutions which work for you. With this book, you will be able to accelerate your learning and accelerate your career.

How to Coach is your personal coach in a book. Keep it handy and it will always be available when you need it most.

Note

1   The original quotation is 'La guerre! C'est une chose trop grave pour la confier à des militaires', which I have translated loosely.

Part 1

Coaching for success

Chapter 1

The coaching discussion: the five O's model

Any coaching discussion is simply a structured conversation. Once you have the structure, you can adapt it to your own style and needs. You can use it to help your team; you can use it with colleagues to help solve problems; you can use it yourself to work through the toughest challenges you face. It is a simple framework and a simple way of thinking. There is no magic beyond a disciplined way of thinking and dealing with challenges.

It is easy to make things complicated, much harder to make them simple. But life is short, so let's make things simple. The structured conversation boils down to the five O's. Once you have mastered these, you have mastered the basics of the coaching conversation. Here are the five O's:

- **Objectives:** What are we trying to achieve, what is the desired outcome?
- **Overview:** What is the situation, and how does it look from different points of view?
- **Options:** What are our possible courses of action, and what are the benefits and risks of each one?
- **Obstacles:** What will stop us taking the best course of action, and how can we overcome those obstacles?
- **Outcome:** Who will do what where, how and when?

And that's it. That is the coaching conversation in a nutshell. If there is only one thing you take away from this book, take away the five O's. The mystique and magic of coaching come down to a very simple framework.

Anyone can use these five O's straight away. But to use them well takes time and practice. After fifteen years of coaching, I have discovered most of the ways of messing up. So the rest of this chapter looks in more detail at how you can put these principles to work without messing up.

Which model?

If you have read other books on coaching, you may wonder why I have not used the very popular GROW (or t-GROW) model, which stands for Goals, Reality, Obstacles/Options and Will/Way Forward or Wrap Up. In practice, both models are very close. There are three reasons for going with the five O's model:

- I find it easier to remember and to work with: you make your own choice on that one.
- Five O's is more explicitly a problem-solving framework which can be used not just in coaching your team, but also in dealing with problems, crises and conflicts by creating clarity out of confusion.
- I want to release coaching from the domain of the professional coach and their precious tools, and put coaching firmly back in the hands of the practising manager: the five O's deliberately create distance from the unnecessary mystique of the profession.

Even within the short description of the GROW model, you will see there are competing views of what it should stand for. Should it be GROW or t-GROW with the 't' for 'theme'? Should O be Options or Obstacles? Should W be Will or Way Forward or Wrap Up? We will ignore all of these debates and focus on the simple, tried and trusted five O's model.

Let's look at how you can use the five O's model in practice.

Even before you start the coaching conversation, make sure you are in the right time, place and mood.

- The right time is rarely in the middle of the day, when you have five minutes sandwiched between two other urgent meetings. A coaching discussion takes time: the end of the day is ideal, when neither party is looking at a watch and thinking about the next meeting.

- The right place is in private. As soon as a third person is in the room, the meeting is a public meeting. You are unlikely to hear real hopes, fears and views aired in public.

- The right mood is essential. If a team member is bouncing off the wall with anger and frustration, the first task is to stop them bouncing off the wall. This phase of the conversation has been inelegantly described as 'getting the shits out'. Let them vent. Let them tell you why the world is unfair, unreasonable and there is a universal conspiracy against them. Don't argue. Pretend you are in a coffee shop listening to some first-rate gossip from a friend: however implausible the gossip is, you do not want to stop them. You quietly encourage them. Only when they have vented completely will they have calmed down enough to have a sensible discussion. This may take time: be patient. You will not hear sense until they have calmed down. In many cases, once they have calmed down, they see sense: they will solve their problem for you.

Once you have the right time, place and mood you are ready to start a coaching conversation. The first task is to find out what the goal is. This game is called 'Will the real issue stand up?' The stated problem is often a cover or a symptom of another issue.

Objectives

The right answer to the wrong question is useless. Your first task if coaching yourself or anyone else is to understand what you need to achieve. I learned this when I was asked to make a presentation to the board for the first time. Knowing how important this would be, I prepared carefully. I had a snappy presentation and over 100 slides of back-up material to deal with any question that could possibly be asked. Well, nearly any question. After I had finished my carefully rehearsed presentation there was silence. Then the CEO coughed quietly and asked: 'What, precisely, was the problem you were solving for us?' That was the one question I was not ready for.

> your first task ... is to understand what you need to achieve

If you have understood what you must achieve, you are well on the way to success. If you do not understand this, you are on the low road to disaster. A few examples will make the case.

- **The monthly report.** A monthly report is not just another piece of routine administration. It tells a story about where your unit is and where it is going. At P&G all new young Brand Assistants were drilled in the art of submitting a bi-monthly report on their brand which would tell a clear story about what was going on and what needed to happen next. You have to decide if your routine report is simply box filling, or if it is a chance to tell a story and to sell a message: if so, what is the message and who is it for? Be clear on the goal.

- **The presentation.** Presenting to a large group can be intimidating. So what is the goal: to avoid messing up; to show off your expertise; to demonstrate your brilliant entertaining skills; to impress everyone; to persuade one or two key executives about a big message? Typically, a goal that is focused on one message and a couple of people is far more effective than the other goals. But achieving that clarity takes discipline and courage.

- **The argument.** Organisations are full of conflicts because everyone has a different window on reality: finance sees the world differently from marketing, for instance. And when you get involved, it can get political and personal: emotion takes over from reason. Suddenly the goals can become confused: is the objective to do the right thing for the organisation, to save face, to defeat the opposition, or to make a friend? Emotionally, we may want to save face and to defeat the other side. Rationally, these may not be the best choices.

- **The purchasing decision** (or any other decision). Should I purchase photocopier X or Y? In theory, this is a rational choice based on speed, price, reliability and quality. In practice, it is a high-stakes decision: no one wants to be the village idiot who chooses a copier which breaks down at the crucial moment. Plenty of other decisions are surrounded by rational uncertainty and political risk.

In each of the cases above, the goals are unclear to start with. The goal is unclear because the issue is unclear. The issue may appear to be rational: 'What should I try to achieve with this report or presentation?' But often the rational problem hides an emotional or political problem. 'If I make this decision will I look foolish? If I back down in this argument will I lose face and look weak? I don't feel confident enough to make this presentation or decision.'

Inevitably, your team member will state the rational issue first. We all know that business is meant to be rational, and it is safe ground for everyone to discuss. But if that is all you discuss, you may be treating the symptom and not the problem. If a child has a spotty face, then the natural reaction may be to use spot remover. That addresses the symptom but will be useless if the cause of the spots is measles. As a coach, you have to get to the real issue before you can have a productive conversation.

Behind most rational issues you can find two types of deeper issue:

- **Emotional issues:** 'How will this make me look? I lack confidence; I don't like that person/sort of work.'

- **Political issues:** 'How will other teams/units react? Can I get the support I need from elsewhere? Am I being undermined and how can I deal with it?'

People are naturally reluctant to raise these more emotional and political issues directly. A good manager will know enough of the background to sense when the rational issue is less than the

> as a coach, your task is to help the team member discover the truth

total story. The trick is to get the team member to identify the real issue. If you tell them what you think the real issue is, there is a risk you may be wrong and miss the point completely. And even if you are right, you, and not the team member, will be the owner of the problem. As a coach, your task is to help the team member discover the truth, rather than for you to tell the truth as you see it.

To help discover the real issue, you have to be able to ask smart questions rather than make smart statements. Often the smartest questions are the simplest. To make the real issue stand up, here are the sorts of questions you can ask:

1   What would you like to achieve in our discussion? What outcome do you want?

2   What will success look like, feel like for you at the end of our discussion?

3   Is there anything else?

4   Tell me more about that …

5   Why is this important?

6   What is stopping you from doing this? What else might stop you?

Questions 1 and 2 are open questions which set the scene. A simple test for this is 'Will we know when we have dealt with the issue?' You have to know what success looks like. If a team member says he 'does not trust the sales department' then that is not something you will sort out in 30 minutes. You need to dig deeper and find specifics you can work on.

Questions 3 and 4 are gentle probes to see if there is another issue hiding behind the first one. At this point your goal should be to gather information and make an informed judgement about what the real issue is.

Question 5 is a good qualifying question: it tells you how high the stakes are. An alternative way of asking the question is 'What will happen if this is not resolved?' You may also find that the rational and emotional issues part company at this point. If there is tension between your team member and another department, the consequences may be severe, in which case you need to deal with it. Or the consequences for the business may be trivial. Separate the business issue from the personality clash: you may need to deal with both, but recognise which is which.

Question 6 is a good way of making the real issue stand up. You are asking to go behind the symptoms which have been presented to you and you are searching directly for the causes. Do not be afraid to ask this question several times in slightly different ways. If a team member has a problem producing a report, it could be because another department is not releasing data; it could be because the team member is overwhelmed with other work or personal problems; it could be that the team member does not have the right skills and knowledge. You cannot deal with the symptom ('I am having difficulty with the report') until you know the cause ('I don't know how to juggle this priority with all my other deadlines').

Create your own list of useful questions. Be patient. Use silence to your advantage. People feel an irresistible urge to fill the vacuum of silence. If in doubt they will fill silence with the sweetest sound in the world: their own voice. And as they talk they will tell you more about what they really think and hope and fear.

Don't worry if you seem to take a long time on this part of the conversation. It is crucial. If you get this wrong, then the rest of the conversation is a waste of time. If you get it right, quite often the rest of the conversation is very simple. Once you have identified the real issue, you may well find that the solution is staring you in the face.

Quite often, this is the only part of the conversation you need. As your team member talks, you will see the scales fall from their eyes. Once they have found the real problem, they find that the solution is obvious. Focus on this part of the conversation: do not let go until you are sure that you have found the real issue.

Overview

One of the great skills of a manager coach is to help people see the world in a different way. We all have our own window on reality. We have to open other windows on reality and invite people to look through them, so they can see their issue from a different angle. This is a delicate task, because it involves challenging people's self-perception.

Most people have reasonably high self-regard. This is useful because it breeds confidence: low self-regard and low self-esteem are not helpful traits in the workplace. But high self-regard can also be unhelpful. It is standard to find that each team member believes that they are honest, hard-working, reliable and cooperative and that they are surrounded by untrustworthy and unhelpful fools and knaves, which includes you, their manager. This superiority illusion is backed up by academic studies. For instance:

- 93% of US drivers rate themselves as above average for driving skill.[2]
- 85% of US students put themselves above average in terms of getting on with others; 25% put themselves in the top 1%.[3]
- 87% of MBA students at Stanford Graduate School of Business rated themselves as better than the average of their peers.[4]

These results are mathematically impossible but emotionally inevitable. We have to believe in ourselves. But this becomes problematic when we think that any problem, failing or conflict is the result of other people and their failings. We all have a natural aversion to admitting weakness or failure. But we have to take responsibility for our own actions. Until we take responsibility, we cannot take control. If we believe that all our problems are the result of a cruel and unfair world, we have the victim mindset. We cannot change a cruel and unfair world: we can only suffer it. If, instead, we take responsibility for where we are and what we do, we have taken the first vital step towards taking control of our destiny.

> until we take responsibility, we cannot take control

So how much should we be responsible for? Everything. If we have a lousy role with a lousy boss in a lousy organisation, who is responsible for that? And who can change that? A key role for the coach is to help the team member take responsibility for their situation. You will not achieve that by telling them. If you tell them 'Well, it's all your fault so you fix it', you may be stating the truth but you will not be helping. You will simply create resentment. Equally, if you try to be helpful and present them with a solution, you still have not helped them. The solution is not theirs and they will not own it. They may or may not feel committed to your solution, and if it fails then it is your fault, your problem and your responsibility.

So the goals for the manager coach in the overview stage of the conversation are:

- Understand the problem completely, from different perspectives.
- Help the team member see the problem in a fresh light.
- Ensure the team member 'owns' the situation: it is their challenge, not yours.

The way you achieve these goals is, once again, by asking smart and simple questions.

Good questions are open but directed questions. An open question is one to which it is impossible to answer yes or no, as below:

Open questions	Closed questions
How do you feel about that?	Does that annoy you?
What is stopping you doing that?	Don't you have the time to do that?
What are your other priorities at the moment?	Do you realise this is important?
Why don't they agree with you?	Did you explain this properly to them?
How can we make that idea affordable?	Isn't that just too expensive?
What is stopping you making the presentation?	Would you like me to get you a speech writer?
What does finance/sales say about that?	Does finance/sales agree with you?
What have you already tried?	Have you tried X yet?
What did you learn from that?	That was a bit of a mistake, wasn't it?
Tell me more about that ...	Is there anything else I should know about?

Closed questions close a conversation down. At best you get a yes/no answer. Worse, you may simply invite disagreement and argument, at which point the original goal of the coaching session disappears very quickly.

open questions invite richer and deeper answers

Open questions invite richer and deeper answers. You learn more. Your team member retains responsibility for the outcome and may start to see the world in a different light. These questions should tease out three different things:

- the real nature of the problem
- how your team member perceives the problem
- how other people perceive the problem.

Avoid being judgemental. There is no right and wrong: there are simply different points of view. My window on reality is neither better nor worse than yours. It is just different. If your team member feels they are being judged, they will clam up. If they feel that they are having an open discussion about different perspectives, you will have a rich discussion. As they start to see the world from different points of view, they will discover potential solutions.

For instance, your team member complains that his marketing campaign is being blocked. He is convinced that it is a winner and has all the arguments to prove to himself that it is a winner. He feels that sales and finance are simply playing politics and deliberately being obstructive. So now you need to start asking the open questions:

- How do sales feel about it? Why are they blocking it?
- What is finance telling you about it?
- Why won't they agree with you?
- What is blocking you?
- How have you tried to unblock it? What happened as a result?

Note that the first time you ask an open question, you may not get a complete answer. Be prepared to come back to the same question, perhaps rephrasing it slightly, until you hear an answer which sounds complete and accurate.

A good way to check for understanding and to encourage more discussion is the art of paraphrasing. Play back to your team member what you think they said, but in your own words. For instance:

- 'So finance says that this breaches cost guidelines for a mid-year promotion?'
- 'So sales are saying that they have already agreed a similar programme for another product at the same time?'

This simple act of paraphrasing achieves several goals at the same time:

- It shows that you have listened and understood what was said to you: that builds confidence and trust in you.
- It helps you remember what was said.
- It encourages your team member to elaborate.
- If you have misunderstood, any misunderstanding will be rectified very quickly.

Most organisational issues get very messy very fast. When you hear 'finance says it breaches their cost guidelines for a mid-year promotion' it is unlikely to be as simple as that. There will be issues about what costs are counted, and how costs are interpreted; there may be flexibility within the guidelines. Your task is to get behind the emotional bluster ('they are being totally unhelpful and obstructive') and work your way through to the facts of the case, as far as you can find them.

Take your time in establishing the overview. If you were a doctor, this would be your diagnosis stage. You cannot make the right prescription unless you have the right diagnosis. In the example of the marketing campaign you may establish the following:

- The problem: you both want a good marketing campaign.
- The problem as your team member sees it: sales and finance are being deliberately obstructive.
- The problem as others see it: finance thinks it costs too much and sales think it is too similar to other campaigns.

Just by clarifying the problem, you have made a difference. You have gently helped your team member see the world in a different way. Instead of challenging their world view, which leads to conflict, smart questions let your team member discover new ways of looking at tough problems.

It is at this point that you need to have your nonsense detector on full alert. Here are the top types of nonsense you are likely to hear, and the language which is its give-away. Your team member does not intend to peddle nonsense, but they have let their mindset and their language get into a dysfunctional place. Your task is to help them discover a better way of thinking about their challenge.

Mindset traps	Give-away language
Groupthink	Everyone says/thinks; we always; nobody does …
Extremism	Impossible, totally, completely …
Catastrophe/helplessness mindset	Nightmare, no way out, let's move on (to another battle/topic), you win some, lose some …
Conformity trap	Must, should, ought to, required, necessary …
Perfectionism	Not possible, I couldn't, not ready …
Copernican trap (I am at the centre of the world …)	I said, I told them, I insisted, I delivered … – no 'we'
Defensiveness: also indicates not taking responsibility	I said she said but they said and I didn't but they should have and I would but anyway he didn't and I then …
Emotion	Watch the body language: from pumping fists to watering eyes

If you accept these mindsets, you accept defeat. None of the language which goes with these mindsets leads to action. They lead to self-justification or to passive acceptance of fate. These are not good places to be. If you challenge these mindsets head-on, you will get a very defensive reaction. That leads to an argument which quickly leads nowhere. The art is to let your team member discover that there is a different and more productive way of looking at their situation.

In each case, it pays to ask specific questions which challenge the assumptions that your team member is making. These should not be threatening questions but open and exploratory questions. The table shows some examples for the different mindsets we just looked at.

Mindset traps	Reframing questions and actions
Groupthink	Who says that? Who have you talked to about that? Why do they say that?
Extremism	Why is it impossible?
Catastrophe/helplessness mindset	If you had unlimited power (a magic wand) what could you do differently? If there was just one small thing we could work on right now, what would that be?
Conformity trap	Why ought we …? Who says we ought to …? Which requirements are you referring to?
Perfectionism	Why do you think you are not ready? Why do you think it is impossible? What would make it possible?
Copernican trap (I am at the centre of the world …)	How does X, Y and Z see it? What do they say?
Defensiveness: also indicates not taking responsibility	So what can you do about it? (Force the focus on the future and action, not on the past and on analysis and blame.)
Emotion	Let them vent, calm down and start again.

By now you may be noticing that open questions are not completely open-ended. They are not a random walk of discovery. A good coach will have a rough mental map about where they want to go. As your team member talks about the problem, you should be thinking about possible hypotheses to test. Your open questions should be directed to help your team member see the world in a different way.

Behind every question, however open, there is a thought. Your hypotheses should drive your questions, as in the example below.

Your hypothesis	Open (but directed) question
I think it can be done: are there real objectors and objections out there or not?	Who is saying it can't be done?
You are seeing this from your own narrow perspective: the other side may have a legitimate point of view	How would the other side see this?
Have you really talked to finance? Are they really being unreasonable?	What does finance think about this?
You can do this: the obstacles are in your mind, not in reality	What is stopping you doing this?
Is this really important? What is the real issue?	What would happen if you did nothing?

During the overview you want to make the real issue stand up, and you want your team member to start seeing the issue from different points of view. You want them to reframe the challenge so it becomes a productive conversation. Keep a sharp lookout for language which may be symptoms of an unhelpful mindset. Use open questions to direct the conversation and encourage discovery.

Before you move on to the next stage of the conversation, make sure that you both agree what the real issue is. Summarise it, and this is where you may want to use a closed question which leads to a yes/no answer. Your question may go something like this: 'So you are telling me that the real issue is X ... – is that what we need to be working on now?' If there is any hesitation about the answer, then the answer is 'no'.

> make sure that you both agree what the real issue is

Try again with a more open question such as 'How do you see the issue ... – what will it be most helpful for us to work on?' Essentially, you go back to the start of the conversation to re-establish the objectives.

Alternatively, your team member may talk themselves into a solution at this point. The clearer they see the issue, the clearer the solution becomes. If you are happy that they are coming to a good solution, then skip the next stage. You do not need to go through all the other options and choices they face. Work on the choice they favour and you like: go straight to the fourth 'O', which is 'Obstacles'. Keep it simple when you can. Otherwise, start exploring options with your team member.

Options (1)

By this point of the conversation, your head may well be rattling with plenty of possible solutions and next steps. As a manager, you would now step in and give the appropriate direction to your team member. You would take the monkey off their back, and they will learn to be dependent on you. You will have taken responsibility, not them. Sometimes, the best thing a manager can do is to shut up. And this is one of those moments. Keep your brilliant ideas to yourself.

It is easy to say what needs to be done. It is much harder to help your team member discover what needs to be done. But the effort is worth it, for two reasons:

- Your team member will 'own' the solution they have discovered and will be committed to making it happen.
- There is a real risk that they may come up with a better idea than the one you came up with. That is a risk worth taking.

There is a danger that your team members may be expecting you to be like the traditional manager and come up with all the answers for them: they may be wanting to delegate all the tough stuff up to you. This will become obvious to you when you ask them what options they see. If they come up with monosyllabic and evasive answers, then you will need to work to make them take responsibility and start coming up with solutions themselves.

The easiest way to find out what the options are is to ask. Simple questions are best:

- How would you handle this?
- What are our options?
- What would you like to do about this?

If you get short and evasive answers, you will need to be more creative in helping them think about solutions. For instance:

- If you had a magic wand, what would be different?
- If you had unlimited power, what would you do?
- How would your ideal role model handle this?
- When you have faced similar situations in the past, what have you done?
- What would you advise a friend or colleague to do in a similar situation?

The magic wand/unlimited power questions are often effective. You allow the team member to forget all the constraints they see, and you let them imagine what is possible, instead of what is impossible. Remember, your goal should be to drive your team member to action and to take responsibility: don't get stuck in analysis, don't get stuck looking backwards and playing the blame game, and don't let them delegate everything up to you.

> your goal should be to drive your team member to action and to take responsibility

In some very tough and confusing situations, your team member may feel that they are powerless in the face of a crisis that they cannot control. This is hard for both of you. The team member may well be feeling more than pressure: they will be feeling stress. Pressure comes from heavy workloads and tight deadlines. The difference between pressure and stress is control, so if your team member feels no control over what is happening, pressure will turn to stress. From your point of view, that means you have to give them a sense of being back in control. It will be too much to look for the perfect solution. And you do not need it. You simply need to find one or two things that can be done right now to move the issue forward: it may be as simple as making a phone call or finding some information. The trick is to create a sense of possibility, of control, and to move to action. Don't let them get stuck in a pit of hopeless and helpless despair.

You will often find that first ideas are rough and ready. They will be incomplete half-thoughts. And that is OK. Your job is not to judge: it is to encourage. By coming up with a half-baked idea, they have taken the first vital step towards action and taking responsibility. If you judge the idea now, they will immediately clam up. However incomplete the idea is, encourage them. Again, simple questions are best:

- Tell me more?
- How will that work?

Suspend judgement. It is possible that what sounds like a weak idea can become a good idea. Even the weakest idea will have something good about it: find the one good aspect of the idea and work on that. This is the art of the 'nice save': if 90% of an idea is rubbish do not waste time, effort and emotion on rubbishing the 90%. Focus on the 10% and build on what is good, not on what is bad.

Options (2)

This is where you part company with professional coaches. Professional coaches do not get involved in content: they will not take sides or suggest or reinforce ideas. At least, in most textbooks on coaching they will not do these things. But you have no need to be a professional coach. You are a professional manager, and as such you should have a view on what will work and what will not work in your organisation. Use your experience and perspective to give positive encouragement to the idea, or to the 10% of the idea which seems to have potential. Simply by giving praise, you encourage your team member to think more and talk more about their idea.

But you will find times when team members are stuck, or are valiantly trying to sail directly into the wind. They need help. You can help, without taking responsibility away from them. You have two tools which can help direct your team member in search of a viable option.

The first tool is to tell a story. Tell a story about when you faced a similar situation. Even better, tell a story of when you saw someone else face a similar situation and recount how they dealt with it successfully. At the end, you defuse the entire story by saying: 'of course, your situation is probably quite different, so the same thing may not work here'. This is slightly sneaky. You are inviting them to contradict you. Most often they will say 'well actually, that sounds like we might be able to try some of that ...'.

They have now contradicted you and told you that they have heard something which might work. The idea is no longer your idea: it is theirs. Their contradiction has transferred ownership from you to them.

Telling a story is neutral. You are not telling them what to do: you are sharing experience which they can use or ignore. You have removed the hierarchy from the discussion: if they do not like the story, they are not disagreeing with you. You make it easy for them to agree or disagree: it is an open choice on their part.

Naturally, the story you pick should be fairly closely aligned to the situation as described, and should contain the germs of a positive way forward. As an experienced manager you should have seen that movie before, and you should remember how the plot develops. You will have seen and experienced most of what your team face, and you should have a good idea about how to handle it. But don't say 'this is how I would handle it ...'. That is traditional command and control in which you take responsibility away from the team. And the team will learn nothing. Your story depersonalises and de-risks the discussion: you give your team member a real choice about whether to accept, adapt or challenge your story.

Your second tool is to use a framework. The management world is full of frameworks and two-by-two matrices. Some of them are even useful. Usefulness is not defined by academic rigour and number of articles published. It is defined by what you have found useful for yourself in helping you frame issues and think about challenges. Be ready to share some of these frameworks with your team. And be open about what you are doing: 'I have found this is a useful way of thinking about this sort of challenge ...'. Then describe your framework for motivation, or decision making, or influencing people, or whatever the issue may be. Finish by asking your team member where they see their situation in that framework. Part 2 of this book rehearses many of the most common challenges you are likely to be presented with. And with each challenge, you will find a way of dealing with it: you will find simple frameworks which can help you and your team member work through the challenge.

As with telling a story, you are not telling them the answer. You are offering them a fresh way of thinking about their issue. Let them work out with you how to apply the framework, if at all, to their situation.

Regardless of whether you are using open questions, storytelling or frameworks, you are working to the same goal: encourage your team member to identify possible solutions and take ownership of the solution. And that means suspend judgement: do not evaluate the ideas yourself. Let your team member do

let your team member do the evaluation

the evaluation. Do not worry about dumb ideas; do not kill them yourself. As you work through each idea, your team member will discard the bad ideas. Unless you have built a team of fools, you should trust your team.

As ever, the best way to help your team member evaluate an idea is to ask simple but positive questions:

- Why would you do that?
- How will that move things forward?

Be prepared to respond positively. At this stage, you are looking for what can be done, not what can't be done. If you start criticising now, then your team member will have learned that having ideas leads to criticism. The result will be that you hear no more ideas.

Once you and your team member have fleshed out a plausible idea, you can do the reality check which is the next stage of the conversation: obstacles.

Obstacles

We have all had ideas which seem brilliant at the time. Then we get back to our desk and suddenly we realise that there is a fatal flaw to our plan. Or we get distracted and lose the idea. One way or another, the brilliant idea dies before it is born. And this can happen in coaching sessions. You and your team member think you have a brilliant plan. And next morning you come back to the office with lead in your heart: you know it is not going to work. You are back at square zero, but probably feeling even more depressed than last time. You thought you had climbed your mountain, and now you have to climb it all over again: it is not an enticing prospect.

This can be very demotivating for your team member. The two of you think you have agreed a way forward. Your team member leaves full of enthusiasm and next day realises that there is a fatal flaw in the plan. Coming back to see you and admit defeat, and having to ask for help again, is loss of face and thoroughly demo-tivating. There is a risk your team member will struggle on in the hope that things will get better, and you will only find out when it is too late and things have taken a very nasty turn.

So do your reality check in real time.

There are three parts to a complete reality check:

1   Identify and remove any potential obstacles.
2   Identify what support will be required.
3   Prepare a Plan B.

The easiest way to identify the road block is to ask. You need to get all the potential obstacles out on the table, prioritise them and sort them out. This is important. By the end of the conversa-tion you need to make sure that there are no excuses. Your team member should not come back next week saying 'I tried, but … I didn't realise that …'.

You have four questions to ask at this stage:

1   What will prevent you from doing this?
2   What else will prevent you from doing this? (Repeat this question until there is nothing else.)
3   Which of these obstacles are the most important?
4   If we deal with these obstacles, will you be able to go ahead, or will anything else get in your way?

The alert reader will note that the last question is a closed ques-tion, which is a sin in traditional coaching. But as a manager, you need to make sure that there is agreement on the way forward: this agreement needs to be explicit. Once you have an explicit agreement, you have commitment.

Now you have your list of potential obstacles, you can problem-solve them. Again the easiest way is to ask: 'How will you handle that?' If it is a tricky problem, then you can use the problem-solving approach of the coach manager: *objectives – overview – options – obstacles – outcome*.

The second part of your reality check is to see what help your team member may need. You need to strike a balance. You should not take responsibility away from your team member. But as a manager, there are some things you can do which your team member cannot do, for instance:

- reassign responsibilities and workloads across the team
- change deadlines and schedules
- reallocate budget
- open doors and set up meetings with key stakeholders.

This is where you need to be precise and consistent. What you say and what is heard are two completely different things. If you say 'I will look into that problem', what will be heard is 'I will sort that problem out'. If you then come back a week later and say 'I looked into that problem and there is not much we can do about it', you will immediately lose trust and credibility. Like a lawyer pleading a case, you can reiterate that you only said that you would 'look into it', and you may persuade yourself that you are right. But you will still have lost credibility and trust, however righteous you may feel.

If you offer to help, be specific. Instead of saying 'I will look into that problem', say something like 'I will meet the head of finance next week and find out what her views are on this'. The two statements may mean the same thing in terms of what you intend to do, but the second leaves no room for doubt or ambiguity about what you *will* actually do. Vagueness is the high road to confusion, misunderstanding and mistrust.

> if you offer to help, be specific

Your final task in the reality check is to have a Plan B. Always have a Plan B. You need a Plan B if your team member cannot or will not deliver. Your team member needs a Plan B if Plan A goes awry. Having a Plan B is a basic management discipline.

I learned the value of Plan B from some elephants. The first time I was charged by an elephant, I had no Plan B: it was a very messy experience. Second time, I had learned my lesson and had my Plan B (an escape route) and all was well. And then I finally learned the best lesson of all: how not to get charged by elephants in the first place.

In business, if you only have a Plan A, you are hostage to fortune:

- You have no backup in case your power supply goes down: you have to hope to get lucky. But hope is not method and luck is not a strategy.
- You have all your data and information on one hard disk. Start praying.
- Your supply chain depends on just one supplier for a low-cost but essential part. Ouch.
- Plan A fails in a meeting and you have no fallback.
- You depend on one person to get you access to a key decision maker: you are now at the mercy of that person

Inevitably, things go wrong. That is human nature. Be flexible and be prepared.

Once you have a plan with your team member, do the Plan B check. Ask what are the major dependencies and risks in the plan. And then ask what you will both do to mitigate those risks. Most of the time, the risks are fairly minor and they should not detain you. But occasionally you will come across a mission-critical risk which you should both resolve.

Outcome

By now, the temptation is to declare victory and move on. You have identified the issue (objectives), you have understood it (overview), you have found a workable solution (options), and you know how it will work (obstacles). Job done? Nearly.

Now is the time to confirm what both of you will really do. Without confirmation, there is a risk that you have both agreed, without realising that you have agreed different things. Be specific, not vague.

Avoid the temptation to summarise. What you say and what is heard may not be the same. Ask your team member to summarise. A simple question is 'So what happens next?' You should have in your mind the textbook answer that you are looking for: don't wait for your brain to be filled by the brilliance and enthusiasm of your team member. If you have a textbook answer in your mind, you will be able to see the invisible and hear the silence: you will hear what is not being said and you will see what is missing. You will be a much more critical and effective listener when you compare the answer you hear with the answer you expect.

The textbook answer is the answer which all journalists are taught to cover in the first paragraph of their article: *who, what, where, when,* and *why. How* is detail which can follow. Force clarity, as below:

Team member says	Clarifying question(s)
I will talk to HR	When and what is the outcome you expect?
I will keep you up to date on progress	OK – when shall we next meet? Or do you prefer a daily email update?
I will get IT onto the job	Who will you get and when will you get them?

By now, you should both be clear about what each of you will do next. But coaching is more than just problem solving. It is also about people: motivating and encouraging them so that they accept responsibility willingly and so that they are truly committed. Hopefully, you will have conducted the coaching session in a supportive manner. How you do this is covered more in the next chapter on the mindset of the coach (Chapter 2). At this stage, if you sense any hesitation on the part of your team member, you may want to ask one more question, which can be along the lines of:

> coaching is more than just problem solving: it is also about people, motivating and encouraging them

- 'On a scale of 1 to 10, how confident/excited/committed are you about this?'

Look not only at the answer (the score) but also the way it is given. There is a world of difference between an 8/10 said with a big grin and enthusiasm and an 8/10 said after some hesitation and said with caution. This is your final sanity check. If you see doubt in the eyes of your team member, just ask: 'So what would we need to do to get that nearer 10/10?' You are, potentially, opening a can of worms. But better to deal with a can of worms now than find yourself in a snake pit next week.

Notes

2 Ola Svenson, 'Are we all less risky and more skillful than our fellow drivers?', *Acta Psychologica*, vol. 47, no. 2, pp. 143–148, February 1981.

3 In Mark D. Alicke, David A. Dunning and Joachim I. Krueger (eds), *The Self in Social Judgment. Studies in Self and Identity.* Psychology Press, pp. 85–106, 2005.

4 'It's Academic', *Stanford GSB Reporter*, 24 April 2000, pp.14–15; via Ezra W. Zuckerman and John T. Jost, *Social Psychology Quarterly*, vol. 64, no. 3, pp. 207–223, 2001.

Chapter 2

The mindset
of the coach

All organisations are hierarchies. To function, there has to be an element of command and control. This can be a nurturing relationship in which managers help and support their teams. It can also be an abusive relationship in which managers look after their own interests and exploit the teams which work for them. Regardless of whether it is a supportive or abusive relationship, it is essentially a parent–child relationship.

The parent–child relationship may have worked in a world of lifetime employment: there was mutual commitment and loyalty which benefited both sides. But those days are long gone. Employers expect you to be passionate and committed, until they decide to restructure you out of a job. And employees are better educated: they expect more from their working lives than being a cog in a machine over which they have no control.

To be a manager coach, you have to be more than a traditional command and control boss. You have to create a genuine partnership with your team, in which you have proper adult-to-adult conversation. That will generate deeper commitment and higher performance than the parent–child relationship which is the basis of the traditional hierarchy.

This adult-to-adult relationship is not a soft option. It requires more trust on both sides. It takes more time from the boss, at least at the start when you are building the relationship.

In the last chapter, we looked at the mechanics of the coaching conversation. In this chapter we will look at the high-performance mindset that you and your team need to share to make the most of the coaching relationship.

The games people play

In 1964 Eric Berne, the psychiatrist who was one of the founders of Transactional Analysis, wrote a best-seller called *Games People Play*. In this book he described three roles which people fall into: parent, adult and child. And even adults can play the role of a child when they are in an organisation or faced with authority.

In each of these roles there are positive and negative behaviours. The 'parent' (your boss) may induce positive behaviour in you, such as commitment and obedience. They may also induce tantrums, sulks and passive resistance designed to undermine the boss and play the system. We may have our tantrum in an adult sort of way: we are unlikely to lie on the floor screaming our heads off until we get our way. But we will play our games to get our way.

In the days of lifetime employment, it was possible to have a positive parent–child relationship in the workplace: the employer would look after you, and you would do what the employer wanted. Those days are long gone. More educated workers are not content to be treated like children in the workplace and then cast aside when the next round of downsizing or offshoring comes along.

Berne suggests that the future lies in creating more adult-to-adult transactions in the workplace. There will still be different roles, and different salaries. But the emphasis is on teamwork and partnerships: everyone has a different role to play and can only succeed by working together.

Fortunately, creating the right mindset does not involve having a dangerous operation in hospital, nor does it involve months sitting on the psychologist's coach. There are a few routines and principles which, when you apply them consistently, will help both you and your team achieve high performance through coaching.

The seven routines and principles are:

1 Responsibility
2 Respect
3 Listening
4 Partnership
5 Questioning
6 Positive outlook
7 Learning and reflecting.

We will look at each in turn and show how you can put them into practice in simple ways that make a difference.

Responsibility

In a parent–child relationship, the parent takes responsibility. That can be easy for the child, but also leads to the tantrums and sulks which come from lack of control and an inability of the child to get their own way. And the same goes with the boss–team relationship in traditional organisations. The boss is the parent and the team are the children. Even if the boss is decent, it is still a dysfunctional relationship which does not release the full potential of the team.

An effective coach manager will change the terms of debate. The team will work as a group of adults, not as a parent with a bunch of more or less well-behaved children.

As adults, everyone is responsible. We are responsible for everything we choose to be responsible for: if we choose not to be responsible for something, we cannot complain when we do not get what we want.

A mugger's lesson

I was mugged at knife-point and lost £20 (all I had about me) to a drugged-up mugger who needed his next fix fast. At the police station I realised how lucky I was. There seemed to be someone else who they were worried about: they kept on referring to a victim. I then realised they were referring to me. I was shocked. If I have ever been a victim, then I have only been a victim of my own folly.

So, was I responsible for getting mugged? Absolutely. I chose to wear a suit at night in a quiet back street and the mugger must have thought Santa Claus had turned up in person with an early Christmas present. To take it a stage further: I had been aware of crime but had chosen not to do anything to prevent it. The victim mindset would complain about how unfair the mugging was. The responsibility mindset learns and takes action. I now avoid walking alone down quiet streets at night in a suit. And I set up a charity called Startup for ex-offenders, to reduce re-offending. We can be victims or we can be responsible. We always have that choice.

The opposite of the responsibility mindset is the victim mindset. The victim mindset takes no responsibility for any setbacks. Even CEOs fall into this trap: read an annual report in which a firm's results are poor. You will read a litany of excuses from the CEO: the one thing the CEO will not admit is 'I messed up': it is always the economy, the weather, the government, natural disasters, 'unfair' competition or input prices which are to blame. CEOs can get away with this: they are the boss, they earn a fortune and they can afford to retire if they have to.

> the victim mindset takes no responsibility for any setbacks

The rest of us have to take responsibility. Only when we take responsibility can we take control. In large organisations, managers are never in full control of their destiny: we rely on other people to deliver; we are subject to decisions which may be taken thousands of miles away without our knowledge. But we still have to take responsibility for our fate. In practice that means we must:

- control what we can, however small it is
- influence those things which are beyond our immediate control
- stop worrying about things which we decide are beyond our control or influence.

This can be a hard lesson for team members who are used to delegating upwards. The coach manager has to keep delegating back down and to be consistent that the team member is still responsible: an adult-to-adult relationship means team members have to behave like adults.

The responsibility principle will lead to some tension. At the heart of the tension is the question: who is responsible for what? What is the team member responsible for, and what is the manager coach responsible for? From that tension should come a productive discussion about who is responsible for what. It forces the coach manager to be clear about how they add value to the team, and it forces the team members to be clear about what they are responsible for.

By reinforcing responsibility across the team, the coach manager is often more demanding than the traditional command and control boss. Provided you do as you are told, you can keep a command and control boss happy. To keep a manager coach happy, you have to do more than obey orders: you have to take responsibility and deliver. In return, the coach manager has to provide the support necessary for success. Being a coach manager is not an easy option.

Respect

Respect is about respecting the person and respecting limits.

There is an old adage that there is no such thing as a problem person, there are only people with problems. This is clearly not entirely true, but it is a useful assumption to make. It is useful for two reasons:

- If you have a problem person, then you have a problem. You are not a shrink and you should not attempt to sort out someone's life for them. You may choose to give them time away from the office and you may choose to refer them to a specialist who can help. But you are not a psychologist and you should not attempt to become one: you are a manager and a coach.

- It makes sense to separate the problem from the person. Problems are made worse by the way people perceive them. It is too easy to see the dark side and to imagine the worst. As a coach, you have to separate perceptions from reality. Once you have dealt with the reality of the situation, then perceptions will change as well.

The easiest way to respect a person is to listen to them: show that you value what they have to say, and show that you are prepared to invest valuable time in them. In a hierarchy, there are end-less ways you can show disrespect for people: don't listen; ignore them; interrupt them; criticise them in public; show impatience; make 'jokes' which mock them; be late for meetings and make them wait. This is where you should apply the golden rule: 'treat others as you would like to be treated yourself'. It is unlikely that you would like your boss to keep you waiting, put his feet on the table and then start texting while you are trying to brief him.

> the easiest way to respect a person is to listen to them

Respect can and should go further. A strong sign of respect is trust. Show you trust your team: be ready to believe what they say; delegate tough and important work to them; don't micro-manage them. None of this will happen overnight. It takes time

to build respect on both sides. Be prepared to invest. The days are long
gone when respect came from having
a big title and a fancy office. Respect is
no longer about status and hierarchy.
Respect must be earned.

a strong sign of respect is trust ... respect must be earned

As a manager coach you also need to
define and respect limits with your team members. It is worth
having an explicit conversation with your team members about
what you will and will not do. For instance:

- We will keep our conversations confidential.
- We will be open and honest with each other.
- I will support you on professional matters.
- I am not a life coach or psychologist and cannot deal with
  those matters.
- I remain accountable for the performance of this group.
- You remain responsible for the challenges you face.
- We will focus wherever possible on solutions and action, not
  on problems and analysis.
- We will respect each other's time.

You and your team members should agree the limits which make
sense to you. Once in a while, review and refresh your contract.
Sustain the trust you need for a coaching relationship.

Listening

Good leaders, good coaches and good sales people all have the
same characteristic: they have two ears and one mouth. And they
use them in that proportion. Many managers prefer 'broadcast
mode' more than 'receive mode': they feel they are not doing
their job well unless they are making points, talking and having

an impact. But the most effective leaders, sales people and coaches prefer to listen than to talk.

People always like to talk. If in doubt, they like to talk about their favourite subject: themselves. In a busy world where most people have neither the time nor the will to listen, the very act of listening builds trust and rapport. And the more people talk, the more they reveal. As a manager, the more you know the better.

In practice, we listen in different ways at different times. When we are in a conversation, we may be listening in one of five states:

- talking over people
- waiting to make our own point
- listening but disengaged
- listening and encouraging
- active listening.

In a coaching relationship, you want to move from talking over people to active listening as far as possible.

Talking over people is scarcely listening and is counter-productive. It is also very common, especially in meetings where individuals are competing to make their voice heard. In a one-to-one meeting with a team member it is completely unnecessary: you do not have to compete with other people to make your voice heard. When a boss talks all over you, it is not pleasant: it shows that the boss really does not care what you think and simply wants to enforce his or her own way of thinking on you.

Waiting to make your own point is the polite version of talking over other people. We've all been there. We're saying something and it is clear that the other person really isn't interested. With more or less patience they wait until we draw breath and then say exactly what they wanted to say in the first place, with minimal effort to relate it to what you have just been saying. You may as well have been talking to a brick wall. It is not a conversation: it is an oral tennis match in which each side takes turns to serve and tries to score a few points.

It's also fairly disconcerting to talk to someone who clearly is not listening: they are fidgeting, looking over your shoulder, checking their watch or their text messages. Their body is present but their mind is elsewhere. They will listen enough to make a couple of points and wrap the conversation up as fast as possible. They have listened, but they have not engaged.

Listening and encouraging is where we enter the realm of the coffee shop. Go to a coffee shop and watch two people gossiping. One person is normally leading the gossip; the other is encouraging the gossiper to spill the beans. Copy what the follower does: the follower never doubts or challenges the gossip. The follower will lean forward, engage, and make the odd exclamation such as 'Really? ... I don't believe it! ... She couldn't! ... Did he ...?' The more engaged and supportive the follower is, the more the gossiper will gossip. In the office, you may not use the same language as in the coffee shop, but you can use the same approach. Show you are engaged, pay attention and encourage talk.

A manager coach needs to master *active listening*. Active listening can be hard work, at least to start with. But it is a good investment which pays for itself many times over. An active listener will encourage, reflect, question and paraphrase. Each of these things takes effort, because they demand full concentration on what the speaker is saying, rather than what you may be wanting to say. We have to suspend our internal dialogue and focus on the other person fully.

> a manager coach needs to master *active listening*

Within active listening, paraphrasing is the key art. When your team member has stopped talking, it is not your turn to fill the air with your own views. All that does is prove to your team member that you had no interest in what was just said. Instead, summarise what your team member said, using your own words. This is a simple discipline which accomplishes several goals at the same time:

- It shows that you have listened and respected what was said.
- If you have misheard, any misunderstanding will immediately be picked up.
- By saying something out loud, it becomes far easier to recall it later on.
- It avoids repetition by your team member: you have confirmed that they have been heard and they can move on.
- Active listening forces you to hear what is being said.

Partnership

The partnership principle is about treating adults as adults. This is so obvious it is routinely missed in most organisations.

Most organisations are still hierarchies. There are bosses and followers at every level. The boss–follower relationship is the same as the parent–child relationship. It can be a good or abusive relationship, but it is not a relationship of equals and it is not an adult-to-adult relationship.

The parent–child relationship may have worked in the days of command and control. But employees are now better educated, have higher expectations and want more autonomy. In other words, they want to be treated like adults. This means that the role of the boss has to change. The boss is no longer the person who transmits orders down the organisation and information back up it.

A good boss has a variety of roles to play, all of which help the team achieve their full potential:

- Select the right team
- Coach and develop team members
- Secure the right budget for the right targets

- Manage the politics
- Manage performance
- Delegate and direct work.

The critical difference is around coaching. The traditional boss will tell team members what to do, and perhaps how to do it. This is the classic parent–child relationship in which the parent (boss) has all the answers and the child (team member) learns to be dependent on the boss. That is not the sort of relationship which highly qualified professionals enjoy.

In a partnership one side does not tell the other what to do. Each side will have different roles. And when they face a problem, they will jointly work out how to solve it. That is more like an adult-to-adult relationship and it is how a coaching relationship should work. No one has a monopoly on wisdom: two brains will find a better solution than one brain.

By embracing the partnership principle, everything changes for you as the boss:

- You are no longer under pressure to know everything
- You run a real risk that you may discover a solution which is better than the one you first thought of: that is risk well worth running
- Your team member learns to be more independent to develop their own solutions
- You encourage your team member to take more responsibility and to grow professionally.

The partnership principle means that you have a team that works with you, not for you. Weak managers will feel threatened by this: they prefer to hide behind the power which the hierarchy gives them. Strong managers know that the way to engage a high performing team is to treat it as a team: you work together to achieve your goals.

Questioning

Smart managers say smart things. Really smart managers go one better: they ask smart questions. They don't just ask team members good questions: they also ask themselves good questions.

Good questioning achieves three things:

● It encourages the other person to talk more and reveal more.

● It achieves greater precision of thought.

● It challenges thinking and encourages new ways of looking at things.

Telling people to ask smart questions is as unhelpful as telling them to say smart things. The goal is clear, but how you do it is not clear. The previous chapter laid out a series of questions you can ask at each stage of the conversation. Most of them are simple. If nothing else, 'tell me more ...' is neutral and buys you time while you think more about what you want to ask next.

Achieving greater precision of thought was also covered in the last chapter: wherever you hear your team member using extreme language, question it: 'never, always, everyone, impossible' are rarely that clear cut.

Good questioning will challenge and encourage new ways of looking at things. This is a supportive, not hostile, challenge. There are two ways you can achieve this. First, you should have your own point of view on whatever is being discussed. Don't let yourself get trapped by the internal logic of what is being told to you. If you have your own perspective, then you can offer your team member an alternative way of looking at the world. Second, you can simply ask your team member what other people would think, say or do in the same situation. And ask questions which turn the negative to positive. For instance:

> good questioning will challenge and encourage new ways of looking at things

- What would the other person say about that?
- If you were in their position, what would you do? Why would they want to help you?
- So there is plenty we cannot do. What are some of the things we can do?
- If you had a friend in the same situation, what would you advise them to do?

Finally, there is one question which coaches should always be asking themselves. This is the James Bond question. Elliot Carver, the media villain in *Tomorrow Never Dies*, tells Bond, 'The key to a great story is not who, or what, or when, but why.' As with media barons and James Bond villains, so with manager coaches. By far the most interesting question you can ask yourself or your team member is *why*? Only when you understand why someone says or does something do you have a chance of influencing them.

The questioning mindset is not just about asking other people questions. A good coach will always ask themselves. They will challenge themselves and force themselves to think more precisely. We have to manage the internal dialogue in our heads well. Buddhist monks spend a lifetime trying to do this by clearing their minds completely: it is genuinely difficult to control our own minds. But as managers, we have to do this.

Go back to the mindset traps:

- Groupthink: 'Everyone says/does ...'
- Extremism: 'Impossible, never, always ...'
- Helplessness: 'It's not my fault ...'
- Conformity: 'Must, should, ought ...'
- Perfectionism: 'I can't ... not ready ...'
- Copernican trap: 'I, me ...', never 'we'
- Defensiveness: 'I said she said he said but then ...'
- Emotion: check your body language.

Question and challenge yourself when you find yourself thinking this way. The trick is to ask yourself questions which are future-focused, positive and actionable:

- 'So what do I really need to get out of this situation …?'
- 'There are many things I can't do … but what are the things that I can do?'
- 'Why are they saying/doing that, and what can I do to change what they say/do?'

As with learning anything, at first this will feel strange and may not be 100% successful. With practice it will become second nature: it makes anyone more positive, action-focused and productive.

Positive outlook

It is hard to command someone to be positive, happy and enthusiastic. And you cannot train people to be positive. If you attempt this, you may well land up with the office equivalent of hapless hotel receptionists who have been trained to say 'have a nice day' to every customer. They mouth the right words, but the rictus grin on their faces says 'please go away and don't come back'.

But equally, if your team is negative and miserable it is not going to perform well. And coaching sessions tend to start on a negative: they start with a problem. And, as we have seen, if someone is in a funk the best thing to do is to let them vent. Let them get their negativity out of the way.

Being positive is essential: the worse the situation becomes the more important it is to be positive. Long after the crisis has subsided and the storm clouds have gone away, people will not remember exactly what you did. But they will remember how you behaved: were you pointing the finger, blaming someone or something, and running around like a headless chicken? Or were you calm, action-focused and supportive?

Fortunately, there are four simple disciplines you and your team members can adopt which will ensure you appear to be consistently positive. Even if in your heart you have fear and anger, it pays to wear the mask of leadership: be positive, calm and in control. The table shows what you can do, and the questions you need to ask to get there.

> people will remember how you behaved: ... were you calm, action-focused and supportive?

Positive behaviour	Questions to ask
Focus on the end outcome.	What do you want to achieve? What is the best outcome from this?
Focus on what you can do, not on what you cannot do.	If there is one thing we can do today, what would that be? What are the things we can control in this situation?
Find the positives.	What can we build on? What support, resources and help are available?
Act the part.	How would you like to be remembered as a result of this? How would you recommend a friend in this situation should act? How would your ideal role model act under these conditions?

These are questions to ask your team members. You should also ask yourself these questions when you are in a tight spot. Simply by asking these questions, you force yourself into a positive, action-focused mindset. You leave no room for the blame game and backward-looking analysis. If your team member is getting into the blame game, ignore it. You can leave the inquest until later. If you start arguing and debating, you quickly go nowhere. If you ask the positive questions and have positive behaviour, you simply squeeze out the negative behaviour.

Learning and reflecting

We are all learning all the time, even if we do not realise it. When we see someone mess up, we quietly make a note not to make the same mistake ourselves. When we see someone do something well, we may try to copy it ourselves later on. Most of this learning happens without us thinking about it or planning it. It is the classic random walk of experience. If you're lucky, you get the right experiences and accelerate your career. But luck is not a good basis on which to plan your career. If you rely on luck you will discover that career is both a verb and a noun: your career may well start to career out of control.

To learn well, you have to learn actively: learn from the team members you coach and learn from your own and others' experience. These are different skills which take a little discipline to master.

> learn from the team members you coach and learn from your own and others' experience

Learning from your team members is a matter of listening. Don't try to prove you are smart by coming up with all the answers. Prove you are smart by asking smart questions.

Learning from your own and others' experience requires some quiet time to reflect. Quiet time may not seem to exist in a hectic 24/7 world. Fortunately, commuting delays and traffic jams were invented specially to create some personal time when you can reflect and learn from what you have seen and done in the course of the day. Ask yourself three questions about any event which went well or poorly:

- Why did that happen, or why did they react that way?
- **WWW:** What went well? What did I do right, and can I do more of it?
- **EBI:** Even better if … What could I have done to get an even better outcome?

These are essential questions to ask yourself and your team members in quiet moments; they are also very useful questions to ask in a team debrief. The whole emphasis of the questions is positive: it is about learning and growing. In particular, use WWW: what went well. Most debriefs and learning are remedial. They focus on WWW's evil twin: What Went Wrong? What went wrong leads straight to defensiveness and evasiveness, which is a desert for learning.

In practice, we succeed by building on our strengths, not by focusing on our weaknesses. The HR systems of most organisations focus on weaknesses and require staff to address them. This is unhelpful: you would not criticise an Olympic weightlifter for poor synchronised swimming skills which need to be remedied: the weightlifter needs to focus on lifting weights. You can help your team and yourself by having a keen focus on what you are good at, and then making sure that you and your team are in roles which play to your strengths. To the extent you have weaknesses, build your team to cover those areas which you are least strong in.

Positive and active learning help you and your team build on strengths and become more successful.

Chapter 3

Coach yourself to success

C oaching yourself sounds as likely as DIY brain surgery. But unlike DIY brain surgery, coaching yourself is simple, practical and vital. We have to coach ourselves if we want to succeed, for three reasons.

1   We cannot rely on external coaches being around when we need them most. Coaches, like buses, are not available when you want them. In the heat of the moment, when you are in a corner and not quite sure what to do, you cannot say 'Excuse me, do you mind if I call my coach to work out what I should do next?' You need a way of quickly coaching yourself to the best outcome.

2   We are all learning from the random walk of experience. If we want to accelerate our journey, we need to make it a directed journey, not a random walk. That means we have to find a way of learning and coaching ourselves to find out how to become the best of who we are.

3   Coaching yourself is a simple discipline once learned: it takes minimal effort. It is no more than active observation, reflection and then practice. We can all do it, if we want to.

You can coach yourself at any time in any place. All you have to do is ask yourself some key questions. The questions vary depending on your time horizon:

- **In the moment:** making good choices in real time

- **At the end of the day or the week:** learning and developing your talent
- **At the end of the month or the year:** managing your career and development.

coaching yourself
... is a process
of continuous
improvement which
will sustain you
through your career

This chapter will show how you can coach yourself to success over these three time horizons. The coaching and questioning process will become a habit which lets you constantly learn what works for you in your context. It is a process of continuous improvement which will sustain you through your career, at all levels and in all contexts.

Coach in the moment

The management day is full of uncertainty, ambiguity and conflict. There are endless moments when you have to decide whether to push or let go; you have to work out how to deal with awkward situations and occasionally awkward people; things go wrong; deadlines loom and there are too many priorities. Some days you seem to surf the greatest waves effortlessly; other days are a wipe-out in which you do your best but the best is not enough.

Most of the time we deal with these small moments of truth more or less on auto-pilot. We do not have to think too closely about them because they are within our bounds of experience. But occasionally we are faced with situations which are at the edge of, or even beyond, our zone of experience and comfort. At that point, we cannot call our coach; we probably do not have the luxury of calling for time out. We have to navigate uncharted waters alone.

These are the moments when we have to coach ourselves, and do it fast.

The first step is not to get lost in the moment. It is very easy to get carried away by momentum. Instead, step back. Look at the situation as if you were an impartial coach: what would the coach see, what would they ask and how might they nudge you? As soon as you step back you start to control the situation. Just as important, you start to control yourself.

In the heat of the moment you do not have time to go through a full coaching session: you cannot slowly work through 'objectives – overview – options – obstacles – outcome', having established a bit of rapport with yourself. You need to do some speed coaching. Speed coaching consists of just two questions:

- What outcome do I want from this situation, right now?
- How do I get there?

These are very obvious questions. As George Orwell wrote: 'to see what is in front of one's nose needs a constant struggle.'[5] Under pressure, it is too easy to miss what is obvious. The first question is vital. Unless you answer it, you will be caught up in the moment; you will not be in control. Two examples will make the point.

A colleague confronts you, and it is not a pleasant confrontation. He is saying things which are inflammatory: his version of reality is not one you recognise. Instinct takes over: fight (aggressive or defensive) or flight (surrender) is natural. Both are potentially unhelpful outcomes for you. You have to step back and detach: ignore the emotion and do not get caught up in the moment. The first question you must ask is: 'What is the outcome I want, right now?' You have several possibilities:

- Prove that I am right and he is wrong.
- Demonstrate to everyone that he is being completely unreasonable.
- Calm him down and find a way forward for his problem.

The first two options are the most common and most ineffective. Even if you prove to yourself that you are right and reasonable, other people may not share your view. And the more you succeed in defeating your opponent, the more you guarantee that you have made an enemy: that is not a good way to secure a solution to the problem. It may not be good for your future career.

step back and detach: ignore the emotion and do not get caught up in the moment

By picking the third option, you both gain the chance to come out of the situation with a solution and with your reputations intact. You will also be guiding yourself towards behaviour which will look reasonable to others. Of course, you still face the challenge of working out how to calm the situation and find a way forward: that is the second and final question you need to ask yourself in a hurry.

The second example is at the other extreme. It is not a heat-of-the-moment confrontation. You have to attend a tedious company conference – it is the normal schedule. There will be some big plenary sessions in which the big boss will stand up and say things which are instantly forgettable. There will be the breakout groups where your thoughts will be written up on flip-charts, reported out to the plenary and then duly ignored. At least there is the promise of a free bar in the evening.

Once again, you should ask yourself: 'What is the outcome I want from this conference?' You may not be speaking, and you may not be leading a breakout group. But there is still plenty you can achieve, besides taking time out of the office. For instance:

- Set up a meeting with some executives who are hard to reach.

- Find out some information from people who had been evasive.

- Have a quiet chat and make peace with someone who has been causing problems.

- Take time out to catch up on emails or finalise a report.

Even the dullest conference or meeting can be highly productive, if you make it so. The trick is to make sure that you follow an agenda which is useful to you, rather than blindly following the agenda which the conference organisers have laid down. By not getting caught in the moment, detaching and asking the 'What do I want?' question, you take control and make progress.

Wanting something and getting it are two different things. A child may really, really want a tree to turn into a giant lollipop. But wanting will not make it happen. We need to work out how we will get what we want. And that is the second and final coaching question you should ask yourself: 'How do I get there?'

In the heat of the moment, it is hard to think clearly. Typically, introverts need time and space to think things through and come up with a solution. Extroverts speak as they think: speaking helps them clarify what they are thinking. Neither of these are useful. You cannot call time out. And speaking before you think can lead to disaster.

Two tricks can help you.

The first is to buy time. The simple 'tell me more ...' or 'I'm sorry, I don't quite understand, tell me more ...' is neutral and buys time. And if someone is venting at you, it lets them blow off more steam. They will quickly run out of fuel, although the 60 seconds while they vent may feel like an eternity plus a bit more.

Second, use the time to coach yourself. If it is not clear how you can achieve your chosen goal, there are a few further questions which might help you find a way forward:

- What would I advise a friend in this situation to do?
- What would my role model or coach do?
- How have I successfully dealt with similar situations in the past?

In each case, these questions are a way of helping you look at your situation objectively and finding the best way through. You may come up with several options. Make it easy for yourself: discard as many options as fast as possible. You do not want to have to choose between more than two options: as soon as you are trying to think about three options, confusion and chaos will prevail. You are not looking for the perfect solution: you are looking for a good solution. When you're working in real time, the perfect is the enemy of the good, because it prevents action.

> you are not looking for the perfect solution: you are looking for a good solution

These questions do not guarantee success, because success can never be guaranteed. But they do increase your odds of success dramatically.

Coaching at the end of the day or the week

Coaching in the moment is about making good choices in real time. Coaching at the end of the day is about learning and developing your talent. It is the process of continuous improvement. It is self-help which lets you accelerate your career.

You can do this coaching whenever and wherever you have a quiet moment: it may be on your commute or on the toilet. Do what works for you. Commuting time need not be wasted: it is not mandatory to play with your mobile doing puzzles, games or text messages. You can use the time to reflect and grow.

As with all coaching, the trick lies in asking yourself a few simple questions. Here they are, in order:

- WWW: What went well? – and why and so what?
- EBI: Even better if ...

- What did I learn from others? good, bad and ugly

- WWW: What went well (again).

'What went well?' is the most important question. You have plenty of bosses, appraisal systems, colleagues and HR types who will helpfully tell you where you have 'opportunities'. An opportunity is a scary thing in business: if it is a business opportunity then it is the sort of opportunity which will be very hard to solve. If it is a personal opportunity

> 'what went well?' is the most important question

then it might range from being a relatively underdeveloped skill to a crushing weakness.

Your commute is probably tedious enough that you do not want to make it more stressful by thinking about all your opportunities. Instead, focus on the positives. Focus on what you have done well and why it went well. You will succeed by building on your strengths, not your weaknesses.

WWW is more than just patting yourself on the back and feeling good on the way home. It is about finding out how you succeed and how you can carry on succeeding. So you need to go beyond WWW and ask one more W: *why*? Why did that work? For instance, it is Friday evening. You are reflecting on the week. You think about WWW and come up with the following list:

- I persuaded the boss to accept my proposal.

- I beat the really tough project deadline.

- I got a nice thank-you note from operations.

If you finish your coaching at this point, you will feel a nice glow inside. But you will have learned nothing. So it is time to take the next step and ask why these things went well:

What went well?	Why?	So what?
The boss accepted my proposal.	I had listened to what she wanted and what she disliked. I had aligned my proposal with her goals.	Invest time in listening. Go with the flow: make agreement easy.
I beat the really tough project deadline.	I had started work early: built contingency. I had asked for support early. I had been careful with time planning.	Planning pays off. Be clear about my own goals, priorities and time management. Don't leave it late.
I got a nice thank-you note from operations.	I had helped them out. I had complemented them in public.	Be nice. Flattery works!

As you can see from the table, the *why*? question naturally leads to the *so what*? question, which should be 'So what should I learn for the future and do more of?' Over time, you will refine your lessons. Some lessons will be about you. Some lessons will be about other people: what they like, what they dislike, how to influence them and things to avoid. And some lessons will be about the organisation: what you can and cannot do; what is and is not valued; what short cuts and risks you can or cannot take. These are not lessons you will find in any textbook or training manual, but they are the lessons which define your survival and success.

Your second question is EBI: Even better if ....

This is where you can let yourself dwell on some of the more challenging moments of the week. And then work out how you could have handled them even better. The format is essentially the same as the WWW format, but you are working on the tough stuff. The table gives some examples.

Tough moments	Why?	So what? (EBI ...)
Team worked late and got grumpy.	Unexpected crisis cropped up.	Set expectations earlier. Plan work further ahead.
Meeting with finance went nowhere.	They had a different agenda from me.	Agree agenda beforehand. Always have a Plan B.
Year-end budget looks tough.	My budget has been reset to meet firm-wide goals.	Keep contingency in budget for the inevitable year-end squeeze, which always happens here.

None of this is rocket science, nor should it be. In practice, you will probably find yourself recording the same lessons time and again. There are some things we know we should do, but life is short and we do not quite get round to doing them. Only when it causes real pain do we learn our lesson. By coaching and reflecting regularly, you stand a chance of acquiring habits which will avoid the need for learning through painful experience.

The third question is 'What did I learn from others?' It can be painful to learn from our own experience. It is less painful to learn from watching others: if they mess up we can quietly make a note not to mess up the same way. If they do something very well, we might try it in our own way ourselves. Learning from others can be positive and negative. I have learned from every boss I have had. Many of the lessons have been very positive and very useful. A couple of bosses have written the textbook for me on how not to manage: but those lessons are equally useful.

When you see someone do something well, ask yourself how they did it. Take care to really understand what happened and why other people

when you see someone do something well, ask yourself how they did it

reacted positively. It is no good mimicking the words they used: repeat their words and you will not sound authentic – you will probably be out of context. Understand the principles of their success, and how you can copy them in your own way. For instance, some of the lessons I have learned from others do not appear in textbooks, but I have found them useful anyway:

- 'Thank you' is a powerful word and too little used.

- Let other people talk themselves into submission: when they have been heard they feel respected and are ready to listen in return. In other words, I do best when I shut up.

- Being enthusiastic is not a certifiable disease: most organisations have few defences against genuine enthusiasm. So we can only excel at what we enjoy.

All of these lessons are what are known as BFO: Blinding Flashes of the Obvious. But knowing what is right and doing what is right are completely separate.

Coaching at the end of the month or the year

Once in a while it makes sense to take stock. As a coach, I find all my clients at some point want to reflect on whether they are in the right role or not. If you do not have an external coach, you need to ask yourself the right questions about what you want to do.

It is easy to get trapped. You have a high salary. You and your family get used to the champagne and caviar lifestyle. Adjusting back to the beer and chips lifestyle simply does not seem acceptable. So, like an unhappy marriage, you feel stuck where you are. And then you are given the assignment from hell and your boss is the devil incarnate. Life looks tough.

You need to know how to avoid career traps and how to get out of them when you fall into them: in a 30- or 40-year career there will always be bleak moments. And your future depends on how you handle those moments.

As ever, prevention is better than cure. So you should take stock regularly. You should manage your career, rather than let your career be managed for you by your organisation.

Here are the main questions you should ask yourself:

- Am I enjoying what I do – and why?
- What are my signature strengths – and where can I use them more?
- Where do I want to go with my career – and what skills will I need on the journey?

'Enjoyment' and 'work' are not words that go together naturally for many people. But you have to enjoy what you do – or at least gain deep satisfaction from it. I have interviewed and worked with hundreds of CEOs and top leaders, and I have yet to find one who is cynical about what they do. No sports or film star dislikes what they do. Performing well in music, sports or business takes huge effort: there will be late nights, missed family occasions and endless small and great sacrifices you make for your career. You can sustain that effort for a few months even if your heart is not in it completely. But you cannot sustain that level of effort for 20 or 30 years unless you have some form of passion, commitment, belief or enjoyment in what you do. If your heart sinks at the prospect of going into work, listen to your heart: you are probably in the wrong place.

If you enjoy what you do, ask yourself *why* you enjoy it. The answers can be surprising. Not everyone wants to dedicate their lives to climbing the career ladder; not everyone wants to be CEO. There are plenty of people who discover that they most enjoy exercising their professional skills in law, accounting, IT, teaching and elsewhere. They want to

> if you enjoy what you do, ask yourself *why* you enjoy it

be truly expert in their chosen field. Others find they want to balance making money with making a difference and put time into non-profit activities. And some most enjoy freedom: escaping the corporate world and taking on the risk and effort of being your own boss is what excites them.

As a practical test, think back to the days in the last month you have most enjoyed. Be specific about what it was you enjoyed and why. Then think back to a couple of darker days. What was the difference? What does that tell you about the sort of context in which you will flourish?

Enjoying things is important but not enough. I may enjoy eating chocolate, but I am unlikely to make a career out of it – although I'm always open to offers. You have to play to your strengths: strengths which will allow you to pay the rent and buy your bread. For instance, I pretty quickly found out what I was and was not good at when I started consulting. Interviewing Thai producers in the tapioca industry, for some lightly disguised industrial espionage, was not my thing. I can do finance but am easily bored by spreadsheets: I would happily invest far too much time in customer facing, operational and people-focused work. Once you find out what works for you, your responsibility is to make sure you

make sure you play to your strengths

play to your strengths. Find assignments which build on what you are good at and give you a chance to shine.

If you only ever do what you are already good at, you will never progress. And take care: do not be too good at things you do not like. You will be asked to do more of the same and you will be trapped.

If you want to progress, look at the people who are two levels above you. Understand what they do, and then decide whether that is what you want to do as well. If it is, look hard at the skills they need to succeed, and what they did in order to get promoted. This may have very little to do with what is in your formal HR systems which will have the normal mix of 'leadership, teamwork, insight, reliability'.

In practice, watch the informal rules of survival and success:

- 'Sell more work to customers.'
- 'Make budget, no matter what.'
- 'Get noticed by top management.'
- 'Never embarrass the government minister, don't mess up.'
- 'Serve your time and wait your turn.'

In several cases 'ethics' might be part of the formal evaluation criteria, but may be ignored in the promotion decision. Make your choice wisely about where you want to go and what you are prepared to do to get there.

Most professional services firms have a simple hierarchy, which is best described as:

- finders
- minders
- grinders.

You start at the bottom as a grinder. You work hard, but quite often this is the most enjoyable work. You are actually delivering the results for the client. If you are good at grinding, you will be promoted to a minder. You will be responsible for projects and for managing teams of grinders. Managing grinders is a completely different skill from being a grinder. Finally, if you are good at minding, you will be promoted to a finder. This is Valhalla, where you become a partner and get rich. And in practice, this means you graduate to become a sales person. Your job is to sell work to clients, acquire new clients, and gain more work from existing clients. It is another completely different skill from either grinding or minding. If you want to get ahead, understand what you are letting yourself in for, and build the skills you need to get there.

Summary

Coaching yourself is the fastest way to self-improvement. You can always be coaching yourself; you can always learn. And the good news is that the coaching and learning are totally customised to your experience and your needs. You can improve without having to follow someone else's theory or style. You do what works for yourself. It is how you become the best of yourself.

> coaching yourself is the fastest way to self-improvement

To coach yourself you need to be able to detach: look at what you are doing and what you have done objectively. Don't beat yourself up and don't be complacent. Just ask yourself a series of questions and then check that your answers make sense. A simple reality check is to ask what a colleague, or your boss or sponsor or partner, would say about you.

When you learn to coach yourself in real time, you will find you become more effective and insightful in meetings and at moments of truth. By coaching yourself at the end of the day or week, you build the skills which will help you advance. By coaching yourself at the end of the month or year, you increase your control over your career.

Note

5 Sonia Orwell and Ian Angus (eds), *The Collected Essays, Journalism and Letters of George Orwell: In Front of Your Nose, 1945–1950*, paperback. Harcourt Brace Jovanovich, p. 125, 1968.

Part 2

Dealing with your most likely coaching challenges

Your coach in a book

Part 2 looks at the most common coaching discussions which I have come across in the last fifteen years. No two people or problems are exactly the same, but many of the same themes keep on coming up time and again.

It would be easy to leave you to work out the best solutions from the first principles outlined in Part 1 of *How to Coach*. Use the principles well, and you should be able to find solutions which work for you. But that is hard work, and it is easy to run up dead ends without realising it. Part 2 makes it simpler for you. It gives you practical ideas on how to deal with the challenges which most people face, and which many coaches find themselves dealing with.

Just as magicians are drummed out of The Magic Circle for revealing their secrets, so Part 2 will see me drummed out of coaching circles for revealing these 'secrets'. Use this section well and it will become your private coach: you will not need to spend up to £2,000 an hour with a fancy coach to work out solutions to your challenges. This book is your patient, uncomplaining coach that can be at your side when you want.

As with any coach, Part 2 will not tell you exactly what to do. Your situation is unique: we cannot say 'turn left in 300 metres' because only you know exactly where you are and where you want to go. Instead, Part 2 will show you how you can think about each situation. It will give you practical frameworks and real-life options for you to consider. It will also challenge you to look at your situation from different angles and perspectives. A large part of the value of a coach, and this book, is to help you see things in a new light.

Because this is a book, we cannot have a conversation. That means we cannot use the five O's model: *objectives – overview – options – obstacles – outcome*. Instead, Part 2 lays out a series of problem statements, which means that the objectives are pre-determined. The overview is likely to be very specific to your context, so Part 2 will only touch lightly on the overview. The real focus of Part 2 is on the options you have and on frameworks for thinking through your situation. Finally, obstacles and outcome are highly specific to you. You have to keep yourself honest in following through on your decision. If it helps to write your plan down, do so. Otherwise, get on with it.

As a coach, I find that there are five main types of challenge which are raised. These are the topics of the five chapters in Part 2:

- Coaching and making the most of yourself
- Managing your boss
- Coaching and managing your team
- Dealing with events
- Coaching and working with colleagues.

You do not need to read Part 2 from start to end. Read a few sample topics to get an idea of how each challenge can be addressed. Then keep this book close to hand and use it when you need it. This is your just-in-time coaching resource: the chances are that the challenge you face will be covered in Part 2 somewhere.

Finally, I am encouraging debate and support. If you have a challenge which is not dealt with here, or if you have a better way of dealing with one of the challenges outlined, then go to my website at **www.leadershippartnership.com**. You will find more resources, including video resources, for you to use. You will also be able to add comments and questions: no one has a monopoly on wisdom, and you can help others by contributing your wisdom and experience.

Chapter 4

Coaching and making the most of yourself

As a good coach you will help your team be the best of who they are. You should also be able to help yourself become the best of who *you* are. If you cannot coach yourself, you probably cannot coach your team. Coaching yourself is great practice for coaching your team.

Being the best of who you are is not about following the latest leadership fashion. It is not about becoming a mix of Donald Trump and Florence Nightingale. It is about finding out what you are good at and building on those strengths. You then have to find ways of minimising and working around your weaknesses. This normally means finding the right role at the right time. These roles will play to your strengths, let you build new skills and position you for your next career step.

The basics of coaching yourself were covered in the last chapter. This chapter will focus on some of the more common challenges and questions you are likely to face in your career. Each section will not pretend to give you the perfect answer: there is no perfect answer because your situation will be unique. But there are common patterns of success and failure, and it pays to learn from what has worked for other people. Each section will give you the questions and frameworks to help you discover what will work best for you.

Based on fifteen years of coaching, here are the issues which come up most frequently:

- How do I get promoted?
- Have I got what it takes?
- I am overworked
- Stress
- Achieving work–life balance
- Exploding head syndrome
- Should I take this assignment?
- Should I go expat?
- Should I move?

How do I get promoted?

This question gets harder to answer the more senior you become. At the start of your career, you live life in a sausage machine. It is pretty obvious what goes in and what comes out. The rules of survival and success are well known, even if it is hard to win. The more senior you become, the less obvious it is what you really have to do in order to progress: no one writes the manual for you on what you are meant to do.

> you need to be *seen* to have done the right things

At all levels, however, there are some universal rules:

- **Do your day job well.** If you have a gold medal in incompetence, you will not be promoted.

- **Have a claim to fame.** It is not enough to work hard: you need to show you have achieved or contributed something over and above expectations. It should be visible at least two levels above you.

- **Tick the boxes.** Ticking the boxes will not get you promoted, despite what HR may tell you. But if you fail to tick all the boxes, you will be barred. It is not enough to have done all the right things: you need to be *seen* to have done the right things. Don't hide your light in a bushel.

- **Find a sponsor or two.** Ideally, your boss is not just a boss but is also an advocate of you. And it helps if there are other senior people in the organisation who are aware of you and support you. Go out of your way to make yourself useful to these people; put in discretionary effort; volunteer to do stuff for them.

- **Be visible.** There are set-piece events where you have a chance to shine: presentations, reports, budgets, big meetings. Prepare for these well and make the most of your moment.

- **Set expectations.** Don't wait to be asked. If you want promotion, then use evaluations to have an explicit discussion about 'What will it take for me to be promoted?' and then keep following up on that discussion.

- **Look and act the part.** If you want to join a senior club, you have to show that you belong. Brilliant rebels may get through, but it is harder for them than for people who look and act like they belong. Watch how people two levels above you act and behave: they are your role models. If you do not like the club, it may be time to sign out.

> if you want to join a senior club, you have to show that you belong

As you become more senior, you still need to do these things. But they are not enough. You need to become more political, more savvy. There are plenty of very talented people who do not achieve their full potential because they prefer not to indulge in office politics. They may be nicer people than those at the top. You make your own choice on that.

At the top, boards do not just hire people: they hire solutions. The story is very simple. It is like one of those consumer competitions where you have to finish a sentence in not more than ten words. The sentence you need to finish is: 'We need to hire someone who will ....'

Possible answers are: 'We will hire someone who will …

- make us much more customer focused
- strengthen our financial controls
- sort out our supply chain
- raise quality to world class standards
- keep the regulators quiet
- forge excellent relations with government.'

This is a challenge. Today the focus may be completely on financial results, and that is how to succeed. Then the CEO is fired because the financial focus means that the customer franchise is being eroded. The new CEO changes the rules of the game, and suddenly it is the customer-focused people who win. You need to position yourself so that you can win in both worlds. That means you need to have enough in your success and work portfolio so that you can build a story which shows that you are completely aligned with whatever the strategic priorities of the CEO may be. And when the new regime starts, you need to market your alignment loudly: loyalty never did anyone any harm. If that means you need to do flipflops every time a new CEO is appointed, then be ready to flipflop.

So you have to be the right solution to the right problem: you have to be aligned with the needs and strategy of the board. You need to do more. You must do the following:

- **Manage your profile.** With seniority comes visibility. There are plenty of people out there who are happy to discuss your weaknesses, behind your back. This is where your story comes in. You need your claim to fame, your story about what you are good at, what you stand for.

- **Work around your weaknesses.** In principle, that means hiring a great team. You need people who are strong where you are weak.

- **Talk the part.** You have to show that you can breathe the rarefied atmosphere at the top. Show that you can see the needs of the organisation beyond your own unit. This is a delicate balancing act: you need to defend your territory but also show that you are aware of the bigger picture. Do not be parochial all the time.

- **Act the part**, as with all levels of the organisation. But the need is more intense at senior levels which are like a club. They prefer intimacy over diversity: they want people who think and act the same way. Groupthink may not be good, but it is a convenient shorthand way of communicating and deciding things at the top.

Doing all of this takes time and effort, which is rarely productive and often vexing. Some people do it naturally, some learn to do it and quite a few choose to opt out. If you know the rules of the game, at least you can decide whether you want to play or not.

Have I got what it takes?

This question normally comes in three flavours:

- Am I building the right skill set for the future?
- Have I got the right stuff personally?
- Am I ready to step up?

Let's take each question in turn.

Am I building the right skill set for the future?

Typically, people need three sets of skills to succeed: technical, people and political skills. You need to build these skills in turn: one follows the other. You start your career by learning a craft (IT, law, trading bonds, teaching). When you are first promoted you discover you cannot do it all yourself. You have to do things through other people. You have to master people skills. And as you reach the heights, you discover politics. You and your unit cannot succeed alone. You can only succeed with the help of other functions, units and groups. You need their support: so you have to align agendas, work priorities, argue over budgets, do deals. Politics is the art of making things happen through an organisation you do not control. Use this to check where you are:

- **Early career:** Craft skills. Learn your trade, whether it is teaching, consulting, law, IT, accounting, medicine or just doing PowerPoint presentations well.

- **Early management:** People skills: motivating, delegating, developing, monitoring, performance management.

- **Senior management:** Political skills: making things happen with and through other departments; trading off your agenda with others; seeing beyond your needs to the company's needs; making change happen at scale; negotiating priorities and budgets; dealing with resistance, crisis and conflict management.

> don't wait until you are promoted to start learning people and political skills

Don't wait until you are promoted to start learning people and political skills. Start learning them as soon as you can. These skills take years to master, and time is not on your side when you are promoted. You have to make an impact fast, which means you need to develop all the skills as soon as you can.

Have I got the right stuff personally?

Every organisation is on the hunt for top talent. As senior managers look for emerging talent, they are looking for more than skills and performance. They are looking for potential. The 'right stuff' includes attitudes and values. With the right attitudes and values, you will be able to build your skills and performance. Performance is a lagging indicator of success. Attitudes and values predict success. I have interviewed and surveyed thousands of managers and asked them how they spot emerging talent. Five attributes of emerging talent consistently came out on top. Here they are:

- **Work hard.** Hard work is relative to your peers. Do you work longer or shorter hours than your main rivals for promotion? Do you volunteer to do discretionary work?

- **Be reliable.** If your heart is 99.99% reliable, you will be dead within a week. You will not be remembered for the 99.99% of the time you deliver: you will be remembered for the 0.01% of the time you failed to deliver, or were late, or half-delivered, or sort of did an OK job. Are you a 99.99% person or a 100% person?

- **Be loyal.** Teams are fuelled by trust: without trust, there is no team. This needs strong form honesty: has your boss ever been surprised or found out things which you should have mentioned earlier? Have you ever gossiped about your boss in private?

- **Be positive.** This is not about smiling and saying 'have a nice day' to colleagues. It is about finding solutions, not problems; driving to action, not wallowing in analysis; and looking at what can be done, not at what cannot be done.

- **Be proactive.** Emerging talent takes initiative and solves problems, rather than delegating everything upwards.

We naturally all think we have all of these characteristics. And on a good day, we probably do. But a good day does not make a career. A career is a

> work hard; be reliable; be loyal; be positive; be proactive

marathon, not a sprint. And we need these qualities all the time: they are especially important when you are having a 'bad hair' day. Those are the days you will be remembered by.

The view from the top is that not many people sustain all of these qualities for long. That is good news. Having the right stuff is not about charisma and inspiration: in all my research leaders have not expected that, nor have they had it themselves. This is just as well. Charisma and inspiration cannot be taught, and medical science has not yet invented a charisma transplant. If we had to have charisma and inspiration, then we would have to be born with it, and few of us would qualify for success. Instead of charisma and inspiration, great leaders need to be outstandingly professional. It is about doing the basics exceptionally well. That is something we can all practise and we can all learn.

Finally, having the right stuff requires resilience and persistence. The difference between failure and success often comes down to persistence. Many people simply opt out: they are talented and hard-working but they simply do not have the resilience to keep going for 20 or 30 years. In that time there may be periods of two or three years which are very rough. Those who drop out leave the way clear for others. The best way to develop resilience is to enjoy your career: the prospect of the good times will help you through the bad times. If you do not enjoy your career, then a bad year or two will break you.

Am I ready to step up?

For many people, this is a killer question. Diligent and honest people want to make sure that they are ready to take the next step in their career. They look at all the success criteria for the next big step and rightly conclude that they do not have all the skills and competencies that are required. This is especially true when people are looking at the last great career leap into a leadership position such as CEO or Head Teacher. Below that level, you may be promoted: progression can be a relatively automatic process. Moving to the top is not automatic. You have to really want it, and you have to go out of your way to get it. The consequence is that many excellent people do not progress to the top, and the blockage is in their own heads.

> moving to the top is not automatic: you have to really want it

In reality, no one is ever ready for top leadership. The buck really does stop with you. Everything changes, even the way colleagues speak to you and relate to you. So if you wait until you are 100% ready, you will wait for ever. There is some gender bias here. Men tend to think that they should go for the job if they are only 50% or 60% ready: they believe they can pick up the rest on the job. Women tend to be slightly more honest, which is unhelpful in the scramble for the top, especially where they face other institutional barriers to success. 92% of women said that the one big thing holding them back from applying for top jobs was confidence and self-belief.[6] Male or female, we should not let real-world barriers to success become insurmountable mountains by adding our own doubts.

The only way to find out if you are ready is to try. This is not as reckless as it sounds. Ask for the promotion. Go through the mill of head hunters and selection panels. If you succeed, that is evidence that you are ready. If you do not succeed, then most good head hunters and selection panels will tell you why. That is valuable feedback: it tells you what you need to do to become ready. And it has the further benefit of building your skills in dealing with head hunters and selection panels: you do not want to be learning that skill when you apply for your dream job.

I am overworked

Overwork comes with the territory of management today. Logically, you have four ways of dealing with overwork:

- Take on less.
- Delegate more.
- Work more efficiently.
- Keep going.

Let's look at each in turn.

Take on less

This is not even thinkable to many managers. It is a sign of weakness. In the short term, you may not have much choice about your workload. But in the longer term, this is a vital strategy.

If we reframe 'take on less' as 'focus on what is most important' then suddenly we transform it from weak to strong management.

Part of the art of management is to maximise your signal-to-noise ratio. There is too much noise in management: pointless meetings, routine reporting and office politics. You will not be remembered for making or managing noise. Think about how you want to remember this year; what will colleagues and bosses say you achieved this year? These are your signals. This is what you need to focus on.

Now take stock of what you actually do over a week. Measure how you use time. Create three categories of time usage:

- **Signal time:** working on those things I want to remember and be remembered by
- **Noise time:** working on other stuff, which may be necessary but is not moving me forward
- **Wasted time:** doing Facebook, staring out of the window, avoiding doing a messy job, making lists and then making them again, getting coffee, sending emails and waiting for replies and generally not doing the job.

When you track your week, you may find that you are in the office for long hours, but you are not focused and achieving what you need to achieve. You have the chance to change priorities and focus more on what counts. Work less, achieve more.

Delegate more

You cannot create more time. But you can make more time for what is important by delegating away everything you do not need to do personally. Delegation is covered in a separate section, but the principle is simple: if in doubt, delegate. Do not be a super-hero. Leadership is a team sport, and make sure your whole team gets a chance to shine. Let them do more. In particular, look at what is in your 'noise' category of work and see what can be delegated from it. It may include important stuff like routine meetings and reports. You may still be responsible for the report and the meeting, but you can ask your team to do the prepara-tion, which will cut your workload by half or more.

Work more efficiently

This is the world of time management. It may help to go on a half-day course or buy a book, but here are the seven main princi-ples of good time management:

- **Have clear objectives.** Draw up your to-do list for the week and the day. Do not lose sight of what is important.
- **Set yourself goals**, even for the next hour or next ten minutes. When you have met your goal, you can reward yourself with a cup of tea, a biscuit, a look at the Internet. This is the world of short interval scheduling: small tasks, quick turnarounds.
- **Break big tasks down into bite-sized chunks.** Big tasks can be overwhelming, small tasks are doable. But even the biggest task breaks down into small parts, such as calling this person, agreeing something with another person, preparing a short briefing paper.
- **Do it right first time.** Avoid rework, which is a big time killer. You have to unpick the work and probably rework expectations with colleagues before you start the work again. Rework does not double your effort: it can increase your effort fourfold.
- **Schedule assertively.** Work the diary to your needs: avoid dead time between meetings.
- **Be flexible.** Gurus tell you that you have to plan your day and have distinct times for thinking and doing. Life is not like that.

Queues and commuting are good thinking times. Keep the momentum up.

- **Do it once and do it now.** Touch each email and piece of paper once. You have some simple choices:
  - ○ *Do it*: deal with it now, make the decision.
  - ○ *Ditch it*: ignore it. Put it in the number one file: the trash folder.
  - ○ *Delegate it*: pass it on to the right person.
  - ○ *Don't delay*: it will only fester and get worse.

have clear objectives; set yourself goals; do it right first time

The good news is that if you are like most managers, you will not be very good at time management. This is good news because it means you can do more simply by managing yourself and your time better.

Keep going

This is the default choice of most managers. They keep going in the hope that they can work through the current storm and reach the clear calm waters beyond. This tends to be an illusion. One storm clears, but then another brews. We can always imagine the clear calm waters, but we can never reach them. Look hard at the work patterns in your office: is this really an exceptional period of heavy work, or is every period exceptional?

Whether you are in an exceptional storm, or a storm as usual, it makes sense to learn to work more efficiently, to delegate well and to focus on what counts.

Stress

Stress has become the number one cause of absenteeism in the workplace.[7] Some of this is down to fashion in illness: back pain, whiplash, chronic fatigue syndrome have all become fashionable for different reasons at different times. They are all hard to diagnose precisely. Although some use 'stress' as a catch-all excuse, for many people stress is real. And there are good reasons why stress is growing:

- The changing nature of work, from certainty to ambiguity, makes it harder for us to have control over our lives, or to know when we have finished work. In practice, we have never finished.
- Technology is hurting by overloading us with information, raising expectations, requiring us to be on 24/7 and demanding immediate responses.

Although difficult to diagnose, see how you score against these classic indicators of stress:

- finding it harder to sleep
- using alcohol, tobacco or drugs more
- increased irritability with others
- more worry, less able to concentrate
- low in mood, seeing the negatives, not the positives.

As with any list of symptoms, you do not have to be a hypochondriac to imagine you are suffering. In practice, you will know when stress is getting to you and it is not a pleasant place to be.

Dealing with stress takes time. Your first task is to regain control of your life. The difference between pressure and stress is control. Pressure is useful: it forces us to perform at a higher level than without pressure. But when we face huge pressure and we have no control over our destiny, then we start to feel stress.

the difference between pressure and stress is control

When overwhelmed by troubles, start by breaking your troubles into small parts.

- What are the things I can control and what can I do now? Even if all you can do is make a phone call, send an email or ask for help, do it. Focus on what you can do, not on what you cannot do. All you can do about things beyond your control is worry, and that does not help.

- What are the things I must do? Then challenge yourself: must I personally do them, or can I get help? Can I slip deadlines? Can I ask someone else to take over?

- What are the things I can ditch or delegate? To regain control, you need focus. Get rid of everything you do not need to do personally. Reduce, simplify and focus.

- Focus on the outcome. Set yourself a time-based goal: end of the week or month. What will 'good' look like? And if you get there, how will you feel? So what do you need to do to get there? Find the light at the end of your tunnel and move towards it.

- Work less. Create space to recover physically. And if you are facing a crunch, then at least time-limit it. Work out when you will be able to find recovery time. If you have no prospect of any recovery time ever, then look at how your job can be restructured so that it becomes more doable.

- Focus on the positives. You are probably in a stressful situation because you are successful and have an important role. You probably have much to celebrate in your life, and much to look forward to. Yes, there may be hard times right now. But these are the times when we learn and grow fastest.

- Get professional help. See your doctor. Your stress symptoms may be covering or causing other problems. Do not die for work.

Achieving work–life balance

Work–life balance is normally a euphemism for working less. And when did you ever hear a work–life balance guru advocating more work? Successful people are often very driven. They are not always comfortable people to be with, either in business or socially. If you crave success, then your work–life balance will be tilted heavily to work: family and private life will take second place.

The reality is that management is hard work. At the start of your career you have to put in the hours to master your craft, make a difference and get noticed. And the more senior you become, the more responsibility and ambiguity you have to deal with. Your work is never finished: if you are an over-achiever, or competitive, or a perfectionist, or just very diligent, there will always be reasons why you should work longer and harder. And the risk is that eventually you burn out and then drop out. You need a sustainable level of effort, which accommodates the need for occasional bursts of overwork.

If you want to move away from the 24/7 work life, then here is what you can do:

- **Focus your work.** Be clear about what you must achieve: where you will make your mark. Most other stuff can be ditched or delegated. Have clear priorities. That means being prepared to say 'no' to the latest hare-brained scheme from top management: you do not have to tilt at every windmill.

- **Delegate more.** This is the best way of working less, while building your team. High achievers have high self-regard, and find it difficult to trust anyone as much as they trust themselves.

- **Compartmentalise your life.** Make sure that there are times when you really leave work: when you do not check emails and answer the phone. These are the times when you can concentrate on your family, your other interests or, if you are competitive, on your sport. Much of the pressure we feel comes from always being 'on'. Find the 'off' switch and the pressure will ease.

> make sure that there are times when you really leave work

Finally, take stock. Work–life balance is a problem, but so are our perceptions of work–life balance. Historically, we are the idlest generation ever. The average working year in industrial countries has declined from around 3,000 hours in 1870 to 1,700 hours currently.[8] However, while manual workers have enjoyed most of that decline, management hours may have increased. Even so, see what your work–life balance is really like: log your hours for a month or so.

- How often do you get caught in a rush-hour crush at 8 a.m. on a Sunday morning?
- How often are you called into meetings which start after 6 p.m.?

You may find that 24/7 exists more in your mind than in reality. You can carve out personal space and time which allows you to relax and recover.

If you are not happy with your work–life balance, it is often a sign that you are not happy with your work. People who are really engaged with and passionate about their work do not complain about work–life balance. If work–life balance is getting you down, look at your work and ask whether you enjoy it as much as before. What has changed? And what would need to change to re-energise you? The three big changes to look out for are:

- change of role: new assignments, new responsibilities
- change of boss: new working style and expectations
- change of environment: new location, office, or working conditions.

It is also possible that time has taken its toll: you have grown tired, perhaps a little cynical, and have fallen out of love with your career. In which case, you may want to think about moving on.

Exploding head syndrome

We have all been there. You are having a 'bad hair' day. One thing after another seems to be designed to wind you up. And then someone decides to push you over the brink. You are about to discover your inner Genghis Khan. How do you avoid doing something which you will regret later, something which everyone will remember you for?

Everyone has a different way of dealing with this. It does not matter what your method is, as long as you have a method and it works. If you have no method, then you will give everyone a moment to remember you by. Here are some of the methods which others have told me work for them. If one works for you, good; otherwise, find your own method:

- Imagine what your role model would do in the same situation and then do it, unless your role model is a combination of Darth Vader and Vlad the Impaler.
- Who is the one boss you most admire and what would he or she do? Do the same.
- Count to ten, just like granny told you to. Let the moment pass. It works.
- Breathe deeply: this is the Buddhist monk equivalent of your granny's advice. Breathe in and regain control of your mind and temper.
- Imagine the other person in a pink tutu. It is very hard to get angry with a fat fifty-year-old in a pink tutu. Not being sick may be a greater challenge.
- Grab your (imaginary) Uzi and splatter their brains over the wall. This is very therapeutic, and you can be sure they will not retaliate. You may even smile as you imagine their brains oozing down the wall.
- Detach. Become a fly on the wall. Look at yourself and your situation, and then ask what you should do. How would you like to remember this moment? Act accordingly.
- Focus on the future. Imagine where you want to be in five minutes' time. What is the outcome you want? Work towards that, rather than getting caught up in the moment.

- Wear the mask. One leader has a leadership mask he wears in the office. Whatever happens, he keeps that mask on. People see the face of a leader: what he thinks behind his face, he keeps to himself.

There are endless creative variations on these themes. Several are not publishable. They all come down to the same idea: keep calm and carry on.

Should I take this assignment?

We learn from experience more than we learn from books and courses. That means we have to get the right experience to progress our careers. The crunch comes at assignment time. Which assignment should we take? What does 'right' look like in terms of assignments?

Your first step is to take responsibility. You can hope to get lucky in the random draw of HR's assignment process. But hope is not a method and luck is not a strategy. Control your destiny, or someone else will. You should actively search for the right role. We will explore how you can do this shortly. Before that, you have to know what to look for: if you don't know what you are looking for, you will not find it.

> hope is not a method and luck is not a strategy; control your destiny, or someone else will

Here are the questions you should be asking about different job opportunities:

- What will I be able to contribute? Am I clear about what my role will be? Will I use and build on skills and strengths I already have?

- Am I set up for success? Is the whole project and department set up for success? Do I have the right resources, right support, right expectations in place? Will the workload be sustainable?

- What will I learn? Will I be able to grow and develop new skills? Will I gain experience which will help me build my career?

- Who will my boss be? Is this someone I can trust? Will I be able to work with them in terms of style? Are they likely to stay or move on? What will my colleagues be like, and will I be able to work with them?

- Will I enjoy it? Does the work and the team look satisfying in its own right? What does my heart tell me I want to do?

- How will this help my career? If I do this well, will I have a claim to fame? Will I be noticed?

- How does this compare against my other options? Which is the lesser of two evils or the better of two goods? What if I do nothing? If I turn this down, what are the consequences? Will there be other options, or will I be forced to take whatever comes along next? Will I alienate key people by turning this down?

Rarely does any role get ticks in all the boxes. You will always have to make trade-offs. This means that you have to be clear in your own mind about what you most want: what counts above all else?

The questions above may seem obvious. They are obvious. But they are there for a reason. When careers go wrong, it is normally because someone is in the wrong role. The obvious questions have not been asked. To make the point, the table overleaf shows why each question is vital to your career health.

If you wait for the organisation to offer you a role, you are unlikely to be given the best choice. You may have a choice, but it will be an uncomfortable choice. It may be 'take it or leave it' where 'leave it' is a career-limiting move. To avoid this, you need to find the right role and ask for it. Don't wait. Queuing is good at bus stops, but not in careers.

> you need to find the right role and ask for it: don't wait

Question	Implication
What will I be able to contribute?	If you can't contribute well, you will fail.
Am I set up for success?	Some roles are career black holes. Avoid them.
What will I learn?	Your career only keeps moving ahead if you build the skills you will need for more senior roles. Build those skills now.
Who will my boss be?	The wrong boss is hell: you will not enjoy it, you will not perform well and your career will suffer.
Will I enjoy it?	You only excel at what you enjoy; you will only sustain the effort if you enjoy it.
How will this help my career?	How will it look on your CV and promotion recommendation? You need visibility and success to move forward.
How does this compare against my other options?	A bad role is better than a nightmare role. Create options.

So how do you find the right assignment?

First, you need information and you need it early. The sooner you find out about a good role, the sooner you can position yourself to get the role. Here is how you can help yourself:

- **Know what you want.** If you don't know what you want, you will not get it. Have a good idea of the sort of role you want. Have a very good idea of who you would like to work for, and target that person.

- **Gossip.** Talk to anyone and everyone. The rumour mill in most organisations works well. Long before a role is formally advertised internally or placed by HR, people will know about impending reorganisations and new initiatives. If you disapprove of gossip, then network – it's the same thing.

- **Head hunt.** If there is a boss you want to work for, make yourself useful to him or her. Put in some discretionary effort, volunteer to help out, show an interest in what the boss is doing. The boss will be delighted to see someone who is interested and eager, and when they have a need, they will whisper in your ear. Job done.

- **Read the tea leaves.** Listen to the boring speeches by the CEO at the annual conference, read the abysmal e-letter updates from the board. In amidst the tedium they will be saying important things about the direction they want to go in. That should tell you where the exciting opportunities are likely to emerge.

Knowing what the right role is and getting the right role are different things. I know I would like a billion dollars, but getting a billion dollars is unlikely unless I accept Zimbabwean dollars.

Here is how you can improve your odds of landing the right role, and how you can avoid the death-trap role:

- **Ask.** This is simple and effective. If you want a role, ask for it at the earliest opportunity. Keep asking; lobby; work out what you need to do to fit the role. If you don't ask, you don't get.

- **Be useful to the right people.** Follow the head hunting rules above. Be helpful to bosses who you want to work for, and show an interest in what they do. They will notice you and be delighted to have someone so eager on their team.

- **Volunteer.** Early-stage initiatives often need some discretionary help to get them going. In a crisis, many people duck for cover and a few people stand up and help out. Be ready to help out on those opportunities which interest you. You will often find you are then asked to take up a formal role on that opportunity.

- **Be invisible.** When there are very unpleasant opportunities and bosses around looking for staff, make sure you are both invisible and unavailable. Make sure you are working very hard and that you are completely indispensable in your current role.

- **Be nice to HR.** If HR staff do not know you personally, then you are just a bit of paper to be shuffled between roles. If they know you and know what you like and dislike, then they can look after you properly, and they will probably want to look after you. Be a person, not a piece of paper.

- **Create options.** Do not bet everything on one boss or one opportunity. Have a Plan B. Be nice to more than one boss; keep track of all the roles which might interest you.

None of this guarantees success. But it improves your chances. As a manager you are responsible for many things. The most important thing you are responsible for is yourself and your career. Manage it well.

Should I go expat?

Everyone talks about globalisation. But most executives are not truly global. They may go to global meetings, work occasionally on global teams with people from other offices, and see global clients. But few executives actually pack up their home and life and move to another country where everything is … different.

At some point you may be invited to go global. Tough decision. There is the excitement of the new venture, huge personal upheaval and serious career implications. The only right answer is what works for you. So here are the cons and the pros of going expat.

Cons

- Huge personal upheaval. Make sure your employer looks after all the logistics of moving house, visas, schools, insurance and so on. You cannot afford to spend your first month in post worrying about personal stuff.

- Culture shock. Some people deal with this by living in a tiny expat bubble, where locals only appear to take notes, clean and serve at restaurants. To make the most of your time, dive into the culture and do not judge it. Some bits you will hate, others you will love. Just accept that different cultures are different. Once you start judging and comparing, you will go crazy.

- Family life. Going expat is OK for the breadwinner who will be immersed in work. The rest of the family will suffer more, cut off from their social networks with nothing to do and trying to rebuild their lives. If you move, make sure your family knows what to expect and is willing to go.

- Expats are expensive and ineffective, at least to start with. In your new location you may face language barriers, you are cut off from your power networks which helped you back home, and you will not understand how things work. You need to learn and adapt fast. Be clear with yourself, your boss back home and your local boss about where and how you are expected to add value.

- Expat life can be addictive. Once you get used to being a big fish in a small pond, it is hard to come back to the humdrum life of cubicle-land in head office. As an expat you get used to the fancy hotels and flights, the freedom, the expenses and the exotic travel.

- You will have no job to return to. Forget the promises made about being able to return. Three years later, the managers who made the promises will have moved on and the promises will be forgotten. Even worse, you will be forgotten. You have to stay visible. Attend global events. Get involved in global teams. Make sure everyone knows that you are doing a great job. And work your grapevine to find out what jobs are coming up, so that you can manage your re-entry to the home office well.

Pros

- Global experience counts in many firms. It is a rite of passage in order to reach the top. And it makes you far more employable elsewhere: you have precious experience which others are likely to want.

- You make money and have fun, which is not altogether unpleasant. Expat packages are less lush than they used to be, but you should still be able to save more money and pay less tax than at home. You should be able to live a good lifestyle and you will have fun if you have the right attitude.

- You get to reinvent yourself. You leave the baggage of perceptions behind you. At home everyone thinks they know who you are. Far away, no one knows who you are. You can decide to be who you want to be. It is your chance to make a fresh start and build new skills. Make the most of this: decide how you want to be seen and then act that way from the start. First impressions count.

- You gain responsibility. Most expat roles involve an uplift in responsibility. This is your chance to learn and grow fast.

The good news is that most of the downsides are known and can be managed. You still have to work for the upsides, but they are attractive. Do your own rational assessment of whether to take the post or not. But do not over-analyse. Listen to your heart. If you want to go for it then you have a chance of enjoying it and succeeding. If your heart is not in it, then no amount of negotiating and structuring a deal will turn it into a success.

Should I move?

Moving employer is a big and stressful decision: it is a leap into the relative unknown with all the risk which goes with it.

If you are thinking of moving, you have to ask yourself the right questions about where you are and where you want to go.

First, examine why you want to leave your current employer. Typically, people leave their employer for one of six reasons:

- You have to leave.
- You hate your boss.
- You dislike your work, and want a complete change of career.
- Family reasons.
- More money elsewhere.
- Better career prospects elsewhere.

Let's look briefly at the do's and don'ts of each one.

You have to leave

This happens, even when employer and employee go to great lengths to pretend that your choice is a voluntary choice. When you are in this position, life can feel bleak and lonely. As ever, do what you can to take control of the situation and make the most of it. Here are the top priorities:

- Try to find your new job before you actually leave your existing one: it is far easier to get a new role if you are employed rather than unemployed. When you are in work, you are in demand and you can spin a story about why you want to leave. Once you are out, you cannot spin such a good story and you appear less attractive to employers.

- Work every angle: your best resource is your own network, so use it. Use head hunters and placement agencies. Reply to job advertisements. It can be unnerving, and humbling, to put yourself on the market and subject yourself to interviews. But the more often you apply and do interviews, the better you get at the process: you do not want your interview for your dream role to be your first interview in fifteen years. Get your mistakes out of the way early.

- Finally, be careful how you conduct yourself. It is easy to feel negative, act negatively and speak negatively. This does not help you. You need to stay relentlessly positive: find the positive lessons from your current situation. Don't be negative about your current employer to any prospective employer: no one wants to hire an employee who is negative and disrespectful.

it is far easier to get a new role if you are employed rather than unemployed

You hate your boss

There is a truism that most people do not leave their company: they leave their boss. This is natural: if you have the boss from hell then you land up with a life from hell. But take care if this is your motive. The corporate carousel keeps on turning. Bosses come and go, you will move, and reorganisations happen. In large firms, eighteen months is about average for the typical boss–employee relationship. Within that time either the boss or the employee goes to a new post. Small firms are more problematic: the carousel is smaller and bosses hang around for longer.

Just as the corporate carousel moves on in your current place, so it will keep on turning at your new employer's. The person you so liked and admired at your new firm may not still be in post when you actually join. You can find yourself suddenly with the boss from hell in your new firm as well.

If you hate your boss, your first and second lines of defence should be to find new openings within your current firm. If that is not possible, your third line of defence is to sweat it out until the carousel turns. If that is not possible, you may need to look at jumping ship to a new organisation.

You dislike your work and want a complete change of career

Up to the age of about 30 it is fairly easy to make a complete change. The first-bouncer routine is well established. New graduates find they hate their first job and want to move. That is smart. There is no point in staying in a career you dislike, because you will not succeed. First-bouncing has no negative impact on your CV, although it can feel hard to start again with new graduates who look and feel so much younger than you, after just one or two years in work. And before the age of 30, the MBA provides a perfect way of changing career. The MBA may or may not teach you much of use, but it is a superb placement vehicle for career changers.

Beyond the age of 30, things get tricky. By that point, you should know what you want and have made a commitment to your career. Things get serious. And if you chop and change every two to four years, you acquire a tainted CV. Employers will suspect either that you cannot make a commitment, or that you have failed at each previous job: it normally takes two years to really find someone out and get rid of them.

If you want a complete career change, it is best to do it either early or late in your career. Early means minimum lost investment and CV damage. Late career changes are normally more financially viable: your major spending commitments (family and mortgage) are hopefully behind you and you may have some savings to support you.

> if you want a complete career change, it is best to do it either early or late in your career

We can all fall out of love with our work. I have met professionals at the very top of their professions who seem to have it all, but hate their work: they have mastered their craft and find that there are no more new challenges. They are stuck in a dull but profitable routine. For some reason, lawyers seem particularly prone to this disease: specialisation means that they become more expert at less and less, meaning that they deal with the same sort of case all the time.

At one level this is a lifestyle choice. You can choose to run a vegan farm or train to be a psychotherapist if you want. But it is worth looking again at your profession. Most professionals gain satisfaction from stretching and developing themselves. There are always opportunities to grow, learn new skills and challenge yourself within your existing profession.

Family reasons

Men find this easier than women. Men may regret not spending more time with their children, but often enjoy the alternative society and structure of work. Most succumb, more or less willingly, to staying at work. Normally, it is the woman who makes the really hard choices between work and family. Having it all is possible if you have a large support network of family or nannies plus an accommodating job which pays for all the help and is not too demanding in terms of time. Dream on.

The only good answer is the one which works for you. This sounds obvious, but it is not. It means you have to resist all the social and family expectations of what you 'should' do: you 'should' go back to work and be a high achiever; you 'should' be a good parent and spend lots of time with your children (quality time is simply a euphemism for little time). To make it harder, the answer is not clear until the family comes along, and the answer may change as the family grows.

More money elsewhere

This is hugely tempting and can be a huge trap. The head hunter calls. You reply and find yourself being courted by people who clearly seem to appreciate you far more than your current employers. And then they offer to increase your salary by 30%:

you now realise how far you have been undervalued and exploited in your current role. Simple: time to move.

But there are some horrible traps waiting for you:

- You find the new place is no better than your current place. There is still the boring bureaucracy and mindless meetings. And there is politics: at least in your last place you knew how things worked. You knew who to call, who could help and who might be a problem; you knew how to work the system and you had your allies and supporters. Suddenly, all of your support network disappears. Your capability has been reduced, but expectations have risen to justify your new salary. It is not a comfortable position to be in.

- You find yourself in a salary trap. You and your family will quickly get used to the increased salary: better car, better holidays, better house. The thought of going back to a simpler way of life becomes unimaginable. And yet you cannot get the same salary elsewhere: you have truly become a wage slave with nowhere to turn.

- Your prospects may or may not be any better. Once you are in the new firm, you have to prove yourself all over again. Your salary may or may not progress as fast as it would in your old firm. A 30% differential can soon be eroded by promotion and a little inflation.

Moving may well make sense, but money should not be the main motivator.

Better prospects elsewhere

We all like to think we will succeed. And on balance, it is better to be an optimist than a pessimist. But you need to calculate the odds.

Starting out, thousands of young graduates join large consulting firms dreaming of partnership and wealth. A quick calculation of the odds shows that fewer than one in ten will achieve their dream: probably 90% think that they will be part of the 10%. They score high for enthusiasm and self-belief, low for analytical rigour: that may or may not be of comfort to their clients.

We tend to carry this superiority bias with us throughout our careers. It is better than an inferiority complex. But if you think you have better career prospects elsewhere, then you may want to ask yourself a few questions before making the leap:

● What is the true competitive advantage of the new firm? To be worthwhile, it should be an unfair advantage which infuriates competition and regulators alike. It is far easier to enjoy career progression in a successful and growing firm than it is to be a hero managing decline.

● Is it in a growing or declining market? Again, growth means more career prospects than decline.

● Do I enjoy the people I meet, and is the culture I have found consistent with what I have heard on the grapevine from media, suppliers, customers, etc.? Use your network, do your research. Make sure it is a culture you want to join.

● What proportion of people stay more than five years? Where do people go when they leave? And why do they leave? These are not questions your new employer will want to answer, but it is worth finding out anyway. You need to estimate the odds and payoffs as best you can.

● Do I really have the skills to succeed? Remember, you will be in a new world cut off from all your old networks of support and influence: you will have to work twice as hard to make an impact.

Finally, there are two one-way leaps in a career: once you have made the leap, you cannot return. These leaps are common, but need to be carefully considered.

● Becoming your own boss, or becoming a CEO. Once you have tasted the freedom, and the stress and hard work, of being your own boss, you will probably find it impossible to go back to working for a boss you may not respect in a structure which stops you doing what you think best. Freedom is highly addictive.

● Leaping off the gold standard. In every industry, there are gold standard firms: McKinsey, P&G and Unilever; Toyota, GE and Rolls-Royce; Goldman Sachs. Head hunters work hard to prize people out of these firms. You will command a substantial premium for leaving. But once you have left these gold standard firms, it is more or less impossible to get back in.

Notes

6 Heather Jackson, *Inspirational Journey*, quoted in the *Evening Standard*, 20 August 2012, p. 7.

7 *The Independent on Sunday*, 16 May 2010.

8 International Labour Organization, *Working Time Around the World*, ILO, 2007.

Chapter 5

Managing
your boss

Your relationship with your boss is the most important one you have outside your family. But it is a very unequal relationship. Your boss can fire you, but you cannot fire your boss. If you mess up, you have a problem; if your boss messes up you will still have a problem. If you have a clash of styles, then you will suffer more than your boss.

Because we do not control our boss, who has great power over us, we often feel stress. But you are not powerless. Coaching is about discovering what can be done, and there is much you can do to manage your boss. You can, and should, influence the decision about who your next boss will be. And there is plenty you can do to influence your boss positively.

This chapter looks at how you can manage your boss and deal with some of the more difficult situations which arise with your boss. The sections in this chapter are:

- How do I manage my boss?
- How do I ask for promotion?
- I don't trust my boss
- I do trust my boss
- Receiving negative feedback
- 360 degrees of trauma.

How do I manage my boss?

Boss problems are very common and tend to be very acute. If you have a problem with your boss, it is normally serious because your boss holds the key to your future.

With your coaching hat on, you will quickly work out how to look at the problem.

First, take responsibility. Your boss may be the boss from hell, but that is your problem, not his. He will probably be quite happy. And he will not change for you. So it is your problem and you have to figure out what you want to do about it.

> look at the world through the eyes of your boss

Now look at the world through the eyes of your boss. You have to answer two questions:

- What does he want?
- How does he want it?

'What does he want?' is normally fairly easy to answer. You will have performance objectives and you will be expected to meet them. It is not enough just to meet your goals: your boss will want to know that you are going to meet your goals. Over-communicate: give them confidence. And if there are problems, tell them early so that there are no surprises.

'How does he want it?' is harder. Each boss is unique. But there are some universal truths about what bosses really want. Having interviewed and surveyed thousands of bosses, here are the five things which all bosses really want from their team members, regardless of what the formal evaluation criteria may say:

- **Work hard.** It is very obvious to bosses who puts in the extra effort and who does the minimum. You can get away with the minimum, but do not be surprised if you go to the back of the queue at bonus, promotion and assignment time. There are no short cuts any more.

- **Be reliable.** Bosses hate surprises, because they are rarely good. Always deliver on your promises; be crystal clear about what you commit to; over-communicate on progress; create a sense of confidence and trust that you are the team's postman: you always deliver.

- **Be loyal.** Bosses forgive many things: bad hair, bad jokes and bad dress sense. But they do not forgive disloyalty. You want a boss you can trust, and the boss needs a team they can trust. Once that trust has gone, the team member normally goes as well. Disloyalty can be as simple as failing to speak up and help out when the team is in a tight spot.

- **Be positive.** If you were the boss, which would you prefer: someone who is negative, can't-do, finds problems, not solutions? Or someone who is positive, can-do and always finds solutions? Simple choice. Which category do you fall into?

- **Be proactive.** Bosses do not want to tell you exactly what to do and how to do it. They expect you to take initiative, sort out challenges and solve problems without relying on them all the time.

Beyond these universal truths, each boss is unique. Some are control freaks, some delegate everything; some love the detail, others take the 'helicopter view'; some are numbers-focused, others are people-focused. These are neither right nor wrong: they are what they are and you have to adapt to them. Let's make that point again: you have to adapt to the style of your boss. Your boss will not adapt to you, and whining about your boss does not help.

> you have to adapt to the style of your boss; your boss will not adapt to you

Start by making a note of how your boss likes to work. What are the three most distinctive things about the boss's way of working?

This need not be sophisticated psychobabble. For instance:

- Mornings or afternoons?
- Detail or big picture?
- Process or outcome?
- Words or numbers?
- People or information?
- Control or delegate?

Now compare that with how *you* like to work. This is where you may find the source of all your friction: you simply have different ways of working. For instance, you may be a free spirit who hates control, is good on the big picture and is better in the afternoon. Your boss is an early-bird control freak who loves the detail. In terms of style, you have a nightmare relationship. In terms of the team, you could be very good: you complement each other's strengths, if you can find a way of working together. That is your responsibility. Make a heroic effort: get up early in the morning; give your boss all the detail that he craves, and over-communicate so that he feels in control. These may be unnatural acts, but they are disciplines worth learning.

In summary, take responsibility for making the relationship work. You are likely to succeed if you do three things:

- You deliver on your goals, and you are seen to deliver.
- You meet the universal needs of a boss in terms of loyalty, being proactive, positive and reliable, and you work hard.
- You adapt your style to the unique way of working of your boss.

There will be occasions when you cannot do this, or you do all this and it still does not work. That is where you need to have your Plan B. Make sure you never depend on just one person for your career. Build your network inside and beyond your current employer. You may need to find a new boss. When you have options, you have freedom. Without options, you are a slave to fortune and to your boss.

How do I ask for promotion?

This question comes up often. It is clear that many people are not good at putting themselves forward. They do all the right things to get promoted, but then they are overlooked while more pushy types get ahead. You do not need sharp elbows to succeed, but you do need to put yourself forward.

> many people are not good at putting themselves forward

There are three times at which you should ask for promotion: at the start, at the end, and in the middle.

How soon should you start asking for promotion? The best time to start is on your first day in your new role with your new boss, even if you have just been promoted. It is already time to ask about your next promotion. Bosses normally like to have a first meeting with their team members to discuss expectations. When a boss says they want to 'discuss' anything it is normally a very one-way discussion: they want to tell you what they expect. Make it a two-way conversation. There is plenty you can both talk about. At some point in the discussion you need to raise the prospect of your next promotion.

Here is some sample language you can use: 'I am hugely excited about this role. It is just what I want for my development. And I hope it provides a good stepping stone to promotion. What exactly will I have to do in order to get promoted?'

This language links development and promotion. The boss will be keen to see you develop: you simply add the logical conclusion that if you develop fully you should be promoted. The boss will prevaricate: no boss wants to be boxed into a corner with commitments about promotion. So you need to push again: 'So will it be clearer to you in six months, at our mid-year review, what I need to do?' The boss will grasp at the straw you have offered: you have given six months' grace to your boss. And in six months' time you come back to the discussion. And you keep on coming back to it until you get clarity. Keep your promotion firmly on the agenda. It may lead to some tough discussions if your boss thinks you are not progressing: it is better to have those tough discussions early than to spend years going nowhere. An early discussion gives you time to take corrective action, if you need.

At some point, you may believe you are ready for promotion. There may not be enough positions open for everyone to be promoted. If you do not ask, you will not get. So ask.

Asking for a promotion makes many people feel like Oliver Twist asking for more gruel. And they fear the same outcome: they will land up outcast and working for a Fagin-type character.

Think about the discussion as a negotiation. That means you should keep three simple principles in mind:

- Win–win
- Interests, not positions
- BATANA: best alternative to a negotiated agreement (Plan B).

Here is how it worked with a teacher asking her head teacher for promotion to head of department.

Win–win

What is win–win about asking for a promotion when there are no promotions available? If you simply focus on the two positions ('I want a promotion' against 'there are no promotions available'), you have a classic win–lose argument set up. No one will leave happy, and it is possible the teacher will leave the school. From your side, you need to find out what's in it for your boss. To do this, look behind the stated position of your boss, which may be that there are no promotions available: look at their underlying interests.

Interests, not positions

Now look at the interests of both sides behind their positions:

- **Teacher:** I want promotion. I also want career development and a salary increase, since I have just got a bigger house and mortgage.

- **Head teacher:** no promotions available. I need to keep a good teacher. I have some whole-school projects on literacy and behaviour which need to be led. I have a tight budget and I'm not sure I can afford to hire extra staff for these big projects.

Suddenly, it becomes clear that there is a deal to be done. The teacher can get big career development by heading up a whole-school project. That is as good as a promotion, if not better. It means the head does not need to hire an extra staff member, so there is budget to give a good raise. Everyone gets more or less what they want.

In years gone by, careers advanced like pawns on a chessboard: straight ahead until such time as you get taken out or reach the top. Careers are no longer like that. Modern careers are more like knights' moves: maybe two steps to the side and one forwards, or even backwards, in search of a more favourable position or a better opening. Do not assume that the only way is straight ahead. It is often worth investing a few years in gaining experience which will accelerate your career later.

BATANA: best alternative to a negotiated agreement (Plan B)

In the world of negotiations, BATANA is the ugly way of saying you need a Plan B. What happens if you do not get what you want? What is your alternative? If you have a Plan B, you will be able to negotiate much more confidently. You will know your limits. Because you appear more confident, you will be more likely to get your way. It is normally clear when someone is negotiating from weakness, or if they are bluffing about their choices. The weak are likely to lose, the strong are likely to win: Plan B gives you strength.

In this case, the teacher had a Plan B. She could become head of department at another school. But she did not really want to move or to leave behind the kids she had been teaching. So it was definitely a Plan B, not a Plan A. The teacher made sure that the head teacher had 'accidentally' found out about her Plan B. The result was that her request for promotion was taken seriously.

Summary

Here is how you ask for promotion:

- **Ask early, ask often.** Set expectations positively on your first meeting with your boss, and then keep those expectations on the table. Done well, this is a positive discussion on both sides about your development and contribution.

- **When you are ready, negotiate promotion.** Use negotiation skills: win–win; interests, not positions; and have a Plan B. Be flexible in advancing your career: be ready to move like a knight, not a pawn. Again, this can be a positive and productive discussion for both sides.

set expectations positively on your first meeting with your boss

- **Finally, ask.** Many people are too self-effacing to ask. It is better to ask badly than not to ask at all. At least put your interests on the table.

I don't trust my boss

Trust is the cornerstone of any relationship, particularly of important relationships like those with your personal partner and with your boss. If there is no trust, there will be no relationship. The split may take time, but it will happen. But take care. Be sure that the real issue is trust, not style. To check for yourself, ask these questions:

- Will my boss make an effort to look after me and my career interests fairly?
- Is my boss fair about pay, bonus and promotions?
- Do I trust my boss to be honest with me, even if I do not like what is said or how it is said?
- When things go wrong, do we avoid the blame game and finger-pointing?

If you agree with most of the statements above, you may have a boss you do not like, but you do not have a bad boss. There is the basis of trust and respect. But if you disagree with most of the statement above, then you have a problem.

The simple but difficult solution is to find another boss, before too much damage is done. When there is no trust, you may be able to patch things together for a while. But then there is another blow-up, a reconciliation and yet another blow-up, and the whole dysfunctional cycle keeps going until either your boss moves on or you move out.

You are in damage limitation mode. Whatever you feel inside, remain positive. Be a role model. Be the sort of person who is very attractive to other potential bosses. You have to quietly put yourself on the internal market, and possibly look at the external market as well. Whatever the provocation, do not rise to it. No one wants to hire someone who is negative, complaining and whining, even if your complaints are entirely justifiable.

Finally, do a sanity check. Are you the only person who does not trust your boss, or does the whole team not trust the boss? If you are the only person, then there may be a performance issue behind the trust issue, and moving boss will not help you.

I do trust my boss

Arguably the only greater danger than not trusting your boss is to trust your boss. You firmly believe that your boss will look after you and your career interests. You are confident in the future. You are happy to tag along with your boss. And then it ends in tears, for one of two reasons:

- Your boss moves on, and you lose your patron. You find yourself exposed after life in the comfort zone when you had not done as much as you could have done to develop your own career. You had unwittingly become dependent on one person.

- You discover you cannot trust your boss. At a critical career moment, your boss fails to back you. You are left high and dry.

Even good bosses will, ultimately, look after themselves first. But research[9] shows that senior management ranks have more than their fair share of psychopaths. These are people who appear trustworthy but are highly manipulative. They know what to do and say to get their own way, but have total disregard or compassion for anyone else. They will lie and cheat: because they've had a lot of practice at lying and cheating they know how to get away with it. They use compassion only as a tool to further their ends when it suits them.

Whether your boss is a psychopath or not, it pays not to become totally dependent on one boss. By all means trust them day-to-day, but do not entrust your entire future to them.

If you can't trust your boss, who can you trust? You have to trust yourself. You have to build the skills and track record to make you employable by any boss. This gives you independence. If you fall out with one boss, your skills and track record will keep you in demand. It has been fashionable to talk about employability, not employment, as the way of the future. This has normally meant being able to hop between employers. But the same idea applies within your organisation. Your employability should make it possible to hop between bosses. Employability gives you free-dom and choice.

Receiving negative feedback

Few people enjoy receiving assessments, because few people enjoy being criticised. People take the criticism personally because it *is* personal. So how do you deal with a review which you suspect will not be entirely positive?

First, focus on the outcome. You want the review to be as favour-able as possible, but you do not want to be seen as a troublemaker who cannot accept feedback. You want your reviewer to leave with a script which says 'You had a mishap (don't we all) and have learned from it and you are clearly growing and improving.' You do not want the script to be 'You have not learned, you are in denial, you take feedback badly and show no sign of improving.'

Here are some basic principles to follow:

- **Deal with the facts.** If you messed up, you messed up. Don't hide. Equally, make sure the reviewer sticks to the facts. Inevitably, there will be questions of interpretation: 'yes, the beefeater project did not go well, but it was not my fault ...'. This can become a long and tedious argument which you will not win. You will simply look defensive.

- **Focus on the positives.** If asked, go through every success in terms of what you did and how you did it. Check that the reviewer accepts and recognises the positives.

- **Be positive about the negatives.** If there was a mess, recognise it. And then deal with it. Show that you have learned from it, and give evidence to show how you have changed the way you do things as a result. If possible, show that it was the exception, not the rule.

- **Focus on the future.** Turn the discussion to what happens next. Explore options but do not commit. You are both

focus on the positives; be positive about the negatives; focus on the future

probably in a fairly emotional state and may not be thinking as clearly as possible. Set up a further meeting later on where you can agree on what steps you will take and what support you will get: avoid making hasty promises which you will regret later.

- **Don't get lost in the moment.** Don't become emotional and defensive. You need to prepare carefully. Work out what your boss is likely to say and do, and work your responses accordingly. A good question to ask is 'If I was the boss in this situation, what would I say?'

360 degrees of trauma

360-degree reviews are useful and traumatic in equal proportion. Let's start with the trauma.

You are a boss. This means that your team is nice to you. They know you control their future, their pay, bonus, promotion and assignment. They do not want to annoy you. So you hear lots of nice things being said about you, which confirms your own opinion of yourself. Life is good.

And then some bright spark in HR decides that everyone should have a 360-degree review. It is done well so that all the feedback is anonymous. That means your team members find the courage to tell the truth. And it is ugly. They dare to suggest things like:

- 'not decisive'
- 'no motivation'
- 'does not support us when things go wrong'
- 'no vision'
- 'does not care about us'.

Each comment is like a dagger to your heart. You have been betrayed. Your self-image has been destroyed. And now you know what everyone whispers about you around the coffee machine. You keep your cool in the debrief with HR, because you have to. But you are mortified. So what can you do about it?

The natural reaction is to blow off steam. Deny the data, show how it is selective, unreasonable, biased and driven by bitter people with bad motives. Many coaching sessions have been spent this way, but at the end of it, the review is there. The inelegant management summary is that the turd is still on the table. Deal with it.

Start by changing mindset. Outrage does not help. The alternative view is that all facts are friendly: they shed light on your opportunities and challenges. Use the 360-degree feedback as a personal development plan. Coach yourself to improve in the areas identified. This is a long-term effort: do not expect success overnight. If colleagues say you have 'no vision' you may disagree. But you need to change their minds: you need to prove that you really do have a vision. Perceptions are reality: if you think you have a vision but no one else agrees, who is right?

> coach yourself to improve in the areas identified

These perceptions count, even if they are flawed. If you want to progress your career, you need colleagues and bosses to have the right perceptions about you. It is not enough for you to believe you do the right things: you have to persuade others that you have the qualities which you know you have.

Note

9   Paul Babiak and Robert D. Hare, *Snakes in Suits: When Psychopaths Go to Work*. HarperCollins, 2006.

Chapter 6

Coaching and managing your team

Managing your team is a core task for any manager, yet many managers are given little or no training on how to do this well. Business schools avoid the topic. If you are lucky, you may have half a day's training on styles of management or on motivation. The theory sounds great, until you get back to the office. You are meant to either know it intuitively or pick it up as you go along. Then we all wonder why bosses seem to be so weak at managing teams.

The challenge is not just for new managers: it exists at all levels. At every level the most basic question is: 'How do I take control in my new role?' Just because you have a big title, it does not mean you are in control.

Managing your team is a huge area which could cover most of management life. Instead of giving you several textbooks on delegation, meeting management, appraisals and motivation, this section will focus on the issues which are most commonly raised in coaching sessions. This is a mix of the common but routine and the most acute problems you are likely to face from time to time.

Here are the topics:

- How do I take control?
- How do I manage people who do not want to be managed?
- How do I motivate my team?

- How do I motivate someone who is down?
- How do I set targets and workloads?
- How do I delegate well?
- Who should I hire?
- Giving negative feedback: formal assessments
- Should I fire a team member?
- How do I fire someone?

How do I take control?

Coaching is not just about solving problems. It is also about making the most of opportunities. When you finally get your long-awaited promotion or you make the leap into a new job or organisation, the temptation is to relax and enjoy your success. You know you will have a honeymoon period in your new role, and you have plenty of time to get your feet under the table.

At best, that is partly true. Your honeymoon means that people will not criticise you too much in public too soon. But they will be forming opinions of you fast: first impressions count. And you will be setting expectations and behaviour patterns from the start, which will be hard to break later on.

So you need to start well: you have to start at pace. You do not have time for a gentle warm-up. In practice, that means you have to take control and make an impact fast in your new role. Easier said than done. So how do you take control in your new role, or in any role?

Over the years, I have found that one simple model helps clients take control. It is the IPM agenda. IPM stands for:

- Idea
- People
- Money.

This is also the agenda you need to follow if you want to start your own business, so it is worth working with.

Idea

You need to have some idea about what you will achieve in your new role. What will be different as a result of your taking over? What will change? How will your new unit be different in 12 or 24 months' time? If you have no answers to this, you are not truly in control.

If we want to be clever, we can call your idea a vision or a strategy. But let's make it simple. You need do no more than tell a story in three parts, which are:

- This is where we are.
- This is where we are going.
- This is how we will get there.

Once you have this simple story, you give yourself the mandate to make changes and make an impact. You have taken your first step to control. It should not be hard to find a story to tell. You will probably have some idea anyway of what needs to change. And since most organisations are always changing, there are always new priorities from top management. Take your cue from them. Work out what your unit needs to do to align itself with top management's agenda. This will help you give visibility and credibility in the corridors of power: it shows that you have got the plot.

> work out what your unit needs to do to align itself with top management's agenda

The simplest ideas are often the best, and can be reduced to a few words. The table overleaf lists some that I have come across.

From these very simple statements came a raft of changes to processes, people, budget priorities, performance metrics and more.

If your idea is so sophisticated and complicated that no one can remember it, then no one will act on it. Simplicity trumps sophistication every time.

Situation	Idea
A successful but chaotic start-up charity that needed to cope with growing large	We will professionalise the organisation.
A large insurance company that had become very inwardly focused and inefficient	We will focus on the customer.
A clothes manufacturer that needed to become flexible to meet changing fashion, while managing a global supply chain	We will reduce time to market.

You could, instead, choose to do nothing. That means you inherit the same strategy and plans of your predecessor. There are three problems with this:

- It may be the wrong idea or plan.
- Your predecessor may have promised that success is just around the corner: you do not want to have to live with that promise. You need to reset expectations fast: show that your unit is on the brink of disaster and only your heroic leadership will save it. Get all the skeletons out of the cupboard fast. It is better to beat low expectations than just fail against 'challenging' expectations that have been set for you.
- By accepting the plan given, you become an administrator of a legacy. You are not a leader. You can survive that way, but it will not help you progress to your next promotion.

People

People has three elements:

- Get the right team.
- Set the right expectations.
- Build the right network.

Make sure you have the A team. The A team will make molehills out of mountains. The B team will turn molehills into mountains and are a recipe for long nights, stress and under-achievement.

make sure you have the A team

Move fast. Once you have lived with a team for six months it becomes harder to justify moving them, unless there are real performance issues. If you have a clear idea of what you will do differently, you create a mandate to change the team to meet your new priorities. I had one boss who managed to promote, move or fire everyone on her team inside a week: no one doubted that she was in control after that.

Whether your team is new or old, you need to set expectations with them fast. Just as you will be judging them pretty quickly, so they will judge you pretty quickly. They will be judging you on how high your standards are, what you are like to work with, and what the real rules of survival and success are with you as their leader. You can set the new expectations three ways:

- **One-to-one conversations.** Take time to get to know each team member. Listen to them. Be clear about what you need and what role you expect them to play, both in terms of performance and in terms of style and how things will be done.

- **Group events.** Much as it is easy to mock offsite events and dull hotels, they can be a very useful way of bringing a team together and setting a new path.

- **How you behave.** If in doubt, watch the feet, not the mouth. The feet don't lie. People will believe what you do more than what you say. If you say the customer comes first and then refuse every customer refund in your first week, everyone will make their own decision about what your priorities really are.

The people you need to worry about are not just your team. You also need to worry about your wider network. The most important tant person in your network is your boss. Managing your boss is covered in Chapter 5. But the principle is clear: align yourself with your boss's expectations. Make sure your boss supports your idea and people moves. It pays to ask two simple questions of your boss from the start:

the most important person in your network is your boss

- What do you really (really) want from me?
- What could I do to really mess up?

The answers may surprise you. They often have little to do with the formal HR system. You may achieve clarity about how you are meant to work, which is as useful as knowing what you are meant to achieve.

Money

Finally, work the money agenda. This is about your budget. Budgets are simply a contract between different levels of management. Top management want you to give as much as possible (your targets) for as little as possible (your budget). Work both sides of the equation: what you give and what you get. Naïve managers accept challenging budgets, because that sounds macho and businesslike. It is also a good way of setting yourself up for failure: twelve months of chasing an impossible target. Be prepared to play hard ball. Agree a budget which is realistic and which you can deliver on. Pad the budget where you can, because you know you will be subject to a year-end squeeze, and any unexpected events are rarely in your favour. Taking over is an ideal opportunity to reset expectations, especially if you have a new plan and a new team in place.

agree a budget which is realistic and which you can deliver on

How do I manage people who do not want to be managed?

The age of deference is over. We now know that people in power are not necessarily superior. Better education has levelled the playing field: we can all feel as smart as any politician or CEO. And the media has relentlessly exposed the failings of those in power. Within organisations, command and control still exist but are under threat. No one assumes that the boss knows best or that the CEO is a heroic leader. This leads to the obvious question your team will ask themselves: 'Why should I be led by you?' And for many of them the answer is 'I don't want to be led by you, but I have to be led by you because of the way the organisation works.'

There are some things you can do which will help you get accepted anywhere. And then there are some special cases. You may have special trouble managing people in the following four groups:

- power barons
- professionals
- loose cannons
- people older than you.

We will look at each of these special cases in turn. But first we will look at the broad principles you can use to be accepted as a manager: to be the leader people want to follow, rather than have to follow. Your four principles should be:

> be the leader people want to follow, rather than have to follow

- Take control.
- Build credibility.
- Work as partners.
- Show you care.

Take control

We have looked at this already in the previous section on how to take control. This is about power. It is not enough to be appointed: you have to take control. This is especially important in dealing with power barons, whom we deal with below. The three main principles of taking control are:

- **Idea.** Have a clear idea about what you will do, and what will be different as a result of your leading the unit. Set expectations about what good performance looks like.
- **People.** Make sure you have the right team in place to execute your idea. Be ready to move people in and out of your team.
- **Money.** Make sure you have the budget, money, resources and management support to deliver on your commitments.

Build credibility

You may well have team members who think they should be doing your job and that it was unfair that they were overlooked. Taking control fast, as above, moves you some way to building credibility: you show that you have what it takes to be a manager.

Here are some of the things you can do to build credibility. See how well you have done over the last three months against each of the following:

- Make some difficult decisions. People, money and priorities are often the hardest decisions. Use these decisions to make a mark. Only when you get pushed back do you know that you have pushed hard enough. If there is no push back, you are probably drifting.
- Deal with a crisis. Crises are wonderful opportunities to demonstrate your leadership capability, and are dealt with in another chapter. The key lesson is that you will be remembered for how you behaved more than for the detail of what you did.

- Show courage by having some awkward conversations. Awkward conversations are often around expectations (we cannot move this deadline; you cannot expect promotion this year; we must cut budget by 15%). Show that you can handle these discussions well and that you are not simply bending to pressure from top management, and you will be taken seriously. Be prepared to set high standards: ask for more.

- Be a role model. Act the part. We all like to think well of ourselves. As managers we want to believe we are positive, proactive, decisive and motivating. What have you done in the last week to show that you have these qualities?

- Match actions to words. No one will really believe anything you say when you start. They have seen and heard it all before. Another boss, another face, another idea: sit around long enough and you and your ideas will move on. Only when your ideas become action will they believe you.

When you start, you need to build credibility quickly. Find some quick wins. These can be purely symbolic acts which show that things are now different: initiate 360-degree reviews; change the layout of the office; improve the vending machines; organise an awayday; set up a town hall meeting. You have endless opportunities to make a mark. Most managers miss this chance: they are so focused on getting to grips with their new role that they miss the bigger picture.

> build credibility quickly ... you have endless opportunities to make a mark

Work as partners

Command and control organisations are built on parent–child relationships: you are the parent and your team are the children. More precisely, they may be rebellious teenagers who have no respect for the adults. These are not good scripts to work on. Change the script: create an adult-to-adult script where you work

> create an adult-to-adult script where you work together to achieve goals

together to achieve goals. Naturally, you have different roles on the team. The main themes behind the partnership principle are:

- coaching, not managing
- solving together, not telling
- division of roles based on skill, not hierarchy
- respect, not authority.

Partnership working is especially useful in managing team members who may be much older than you. Seek advice: use the knowledge, wisdom and experience of your team. Quietly flatter them and their capability: let them act as the kindly uncle or aunt who is supporting you. You do not have to pretend to know it all.

When you start, you need to establish the partner idea fast. The best way to do this is to drink tea. Take time with all of your team members over tea (or coffee, if you must). Listen to them. Role-model the behaviour of the coach manager. And then follow up: show you have listened by acting on some of the ideas you have heard. You will quickly become not just a respected partner, but also a leader people want to follow.

There are times when partnerships break down: assessments and assignments are when the hierarchy reasserts itself. Even here you can consult, but in the end you have to decide.

Show you care

By now you will be familiar with the answer to the question 'How do I show I care?' Coach yourself. Reflect on those bosses who have shown that they truly cared for you. What did they do to make you feel valued and respected? Here are a few ideas to get you going:

- Invest time with each of your team members: understand their hopes and fears, their strengths and weaknesses.

- Show you appreciate their work: make sure you recognise each of them for what they do. Build on the positives; avoid any criticism, at least in public.

- Surprise them: once in a while, go above and beyond. Find an excuse for a celebration – something more than one of those standard office rituals like a round-robin card that everyone has to sign for a birthday/leaving do/birth of a child, etc. It should be unexpected but relevant to the success of the team.

As with all principles, these are fine as far as they go. But they never go far enough. Most coaching challenges are far more specific. This is no exception. So let's look at the four specific cases we set out at the start of this section:

- power barons
- professionals
- loose cannons
- people older than you.

Power barons

These are common at higher levels of an organisation. The higher you go, the more powerful they become. The typical power baron will be successful, and they will use that success to create a fiefdom which they jealously guard. They will not let you interfere with their territory, and you cannot manage them.

You have a digital choice with power barons: live with them or crush them. There is not much in between. And you do not want to take them on and lose: then you become a lame-duck leader with no respect and no power.

If you want an easy life, live with the power barons. They are successful and they know that if they want to stay independent, they have to keep on delivering the results – although they have a nasty habit of playing hard ball at budget time and securing an easy budget: this lets them beat budget, look good and get big bonuses for everyone.

If you opt to live with the power barons, you will not be in control. The power barons may deliver results, but they have an effective veto over any changes you want to make. This means that each initiative you want to start leads to prolonged political battles with your power barons. These battles are messy and lead to messy outcomes.

The alternative is to crush the power barons. The best way to do this is fast. Within a month of taking over, reorganise. You do not have to fire any power barons: you just move all the fiefdoms around.

For instance, one executive was put in charge of European IT consulting. The power barons were geographically based (representing Italy, Germany, etc.). So the executive decided to reorganise around industry groups (telecoms, financial services, etc.). There is always a legitimate business reason for this, such as getting closer to the customer, building industry knowledge or deepening functional skills. That is strictly PR. The real purpose was to break the power of the barons. The head of Germany suddenly found that she was in charge of Financial Services across Europe. She was cut off from her power base. She quickly became an enthusiast forcing pan-European changes on Germany, which she had been protecting until a week ago. Her power was broken and the boss was back in control.

Professionals

Most professionals are highly educated and highly skilled. They really do not like to be managed. The whole idea of management is anathema in many law firms. In such firms, real power is with the partners who have the big clients. If cash is king, then the client is emperor. I have heard the CEO of one such firm being referred to openly as the 'chief clerk'. Managers are second-rate citizens compared to the rainmakers who bring in the clients and bring in the cash.

> professionals are easy to manage: just don't manage them too much

Fortunately, professionals are easy to manage: just don't manage them too much. They tend to be over-achievers, so let them over-achieve. If you are a professional, think about how you like to be managed. The main do's and don'ts are:

- Stretch them. Let them over-achieve. A bored professional is grumpy and dangerous.

- Manage By Walking Away (MBWA). This turns on its head the received wisdom, which is that MBWA is management by walking around and keeping your finger on the pulse. Professionals hate being micro-managed. Set clear goals, but do not interfere with the process of how they get there.

- Set clear expectations. Freddie Mercury sang 'I want it all and I want it now'[10] but that was a generation ago. Now professionals want more and they want it faster. Set clear boundaries and be consistent in what you say: leave no room for misinterpretation. Professionals tend to hear what they want to hear, not what you think you said.

- Never demean them in public, even if they have messed up. Professionals tend to be brittle: they look strong but break easily. They have large but fragile egos and can be thin skinned. Criticism does not go down well with their high self-image.

- Make them feel valued and important. Ensure that they understand how vital their work is to the success of the whole organisation, even if it is quite mundane. They need to know that they are doing worthwhile work. Don't just assign work to them: sell it to them so that they feel excited about it.

Loose cannons

We are all individuals, but some of us are more individualistic than others. Loose cannons may be brilliant, but they find it hard to conform. They do not like bureaucracy, rules and procedures. Their natural habitat is in creative industries: media, advertising and parts of IT. At its extreme you have the pop divas who like to make absurd demands: my dressing room must have a bowl of M&M's with all the brown M&M's removed.

Decide whether you want to manage these people at all. You probably do not want them in charge of safety at a nuclear plant. But if they are the star of a global rock tour, you put up with whatever nonsense they want. In between, there are many shades of grey. The main trade-off is between performance and demands: the more they want, the better they have to perform. The loose cannons see it the other way: the better they perform, the more they can demand and do things their own way. They will always push limits and push your tolerance.

Beyond this obvious trade-off, you have to look at their effect on the whole team. In the right industry, they may be inspiring to others. In the wrong industry, they simply set the wrong style.

Your first choice is whether you want to keep or lose the loose cannon. If you choose to keep them, then the principles of managing them are the same as managing professionals: you simply have to take each principle further. So setting expectations becomes setting clear limits: let them fool around within the limits, but they have to deliver when the time comes. Rock stars can do pretty much what they want, but when the time comes they have to get on stage and deliver.

People older than you

This used not to be a problem. Organisations used to have a seniority system: you had to serve your time before you got a shot at moving up. That meant senior people were older than junior people and the whole parent–child script was neatly reinforced.

The good news is that you do not have to serve time. Merit, with political savvy and good performance, will get you promoted.

The bad news is that you might be managing your mother and father in age terms. This is tough for both sides. You may well have no experience or role models to draw on: you cannot coach yourself to success here. To make things harder, you may well have been put in place because the older team members are seen as too conservative, perhaps a bit jaded and cynical, and you are expected to shake things up. They will have seen it all before, and if you go in trumpeting how you will change them, you will fail.

Here are some of the do's and don'ts from experience:

- Make them your allies. Ask for their advice. Recognise and value their greater experience. By asking for advice you flatter them, not threaten them. They will warm to you. And just listen: they have stories to tell and you can learn from them. By listening, you build rapport.

- Ask them for help in making things happen. In particular, ask each one in private to help role-model the new way of doing things. This will enhance their self-image as people with influence. And if you can get them to behave differently, everyone will sit up and take notice.

- Sell your decisions. Do not expect these people to leap with joy every time you make a decision. If you want them to do something, take time to explain why you made the decision, why it is important, and what you need them to do. Flatter them by showing that their role is vital. And keep listening to any concerns they may have.

- Listen and consult. Invest time with each person: show respect. Understand what they want and do not want. Act on any small suggestions so that they see you are responsive to them.

● Take control, as outlined previously. You may be young, but you are in charge for a reason. You cannot afford to get hijacked by your own team. Be ready to stretch and challenge them as you need. You will build respect by taking control; if you attempt to build popularity you will build weakness.

> you have been appointed to make a difference, so ... be bold and set a new direction or new targets

Finally, be brave. You have been appointed to make a difference. So make a difference. Be bold and set a new direction or new targets. If you do it well, you will find that you re-energise and re-engage your older team members. You will be a breath of fresh air and they will want to help you succeed.

How do I motivate my team?

There is a vast motivational industry out there, and endless papers have been written on the theory of motivation. But with your coaching hat on, you should be able to work the answers out for yourself.

Think about the times when you have felt most motivated:

● How did your boss behave?

● What sort of work were you doing?

● What were your colleagues like?

● How much recognition did you get for your work?

● Were your hours long or short?

Once you have your list, compare that to how you behave as a boss, and the sort of work and recognition your team members receive. Be honest with yourself. If there are gaps, fill them.

In practice, you and your team probably feel highly motivated if they can agree with all of these four statements:

- My boss cares for me and my career.
- I am doing worthwhile work.
- I am recognised for my work.
- I work in a worthwhile organisation.

As a manager, you can control or influence the answers to all these statements. Let's look at each in turn.

My boss cares for me and my career

This is the single biggest predictor of whether a boss is seen to be a good boss. If all you do is to show you care, you will be well on the way to being seen as a good boss.

Caring does not mean courting popularity. It means understanding and respecting the aspirations, and fears, of each of your team members. It means setting expectations very clearly: do not promise anything you cannot deliver. It may mean having difficult but constructive conversations about performance. Have these conversations early so that your team member has time to take action before the annual review.

Doing this takes time. This is not time spent, it is time invested. By showing you care for and respect each team member, you build loyalty and commitment which will pay dividends in terms of loyalty and performance.

> care for and respect each team member … build loyalty and commitment

One manager showed she cared for a virtual team spread around the country by going on a tea offensive. The simple act of going to each site, sitting down with staff over a cup of tea and listening to their ideas and concerns converted her from an unknown new face to a leader they wanted to follow. And when she respected them by putting some of their ideas into practice, loyalty was assured.

I am doing worthwhile work

Think back to what you have regarded as worthwhile work. That is the sort of work your team wants. Worthwhile work may well be challenging and stretching. It may mean working long hours: short hours do not motivate.

There is plenty in the management day which is dull, repetitive and unproductive. And if all management was like that, we would all go and do something else. As a manager you have to balance the routine rubbish with the challenging and interesting work.

I am recognised for my work

Recognition is cheap, easy and much under-used. We tend to take people and performance for granted, until they mess up. Most performance feedback is negative, not positive. Again, think of the managers whom you have most wanted to work for: they probably were not the ones who took all the credit for any good work and delegated all the blame.

Recognition is as simple as 'thank you'. How many times have you thanked any of your team in the last 24 hours? How many times have you praised a contribution in public or private in the last 24 hours?

make sure you spread praise around ... and make your praise real

Praise can be done well or poorly. Make sure you spread praise around. If you always praise one half of your team and not the other half, you will foment a small civil war and seething resentment. And make your praise real. Avoid habitually making synthetic compliments that your team know are meaningless. When you find something to praise, make it specific and personal.

I work in a worthwhile organisation

Some of the highest performing and highest regarded organisations have the worst pay and the worst conditions. But everyone in such organisations believes that they are working for a worthwhile cause.

As a manager there is not much you can do about the organisation which employs you. But you can make sure that there is pride in your unit. Set high expectations; make sure everyone realises that their work is vital to the success of the whole organisation; build team spirit and *esprit de corps*. Again, think back to when you thought you had real pride in a team you worked in: what did the boss do to build that sense of pride and commitment? You do not need to reinvent management theory: copy what you know works from your own experience.

How do I motivate someone who is down?

You may be doing a good job at motivating the team. But then you notice that one person is down. Before charging in, take time to check whether there is an obvious problem which can be solved.

If you want to find the problem, first look in the mirror. You may be doing a good job with the team as a whole, but are you treating this one individual differently? Are you treating them better or worse than the rest of the team? Do you criticise, praise, trust and delegate to them as much as the rest of your team? How do they feel against the four motivation statements we have just covered?

- My boss cares for me and my career.
- I am doing worthwhile work.
- I am recognised for my work.
- I work in a worthwhile organisation.

If you are lavish with praise for nine team members but always forget to praise the tenth, do not be surprised if you have one very disgruntled member of your team.

Second, check whether the demotivated team member is always like that. Some people are grumps. They can be good at the job; they can be diligent, honest and reliable. But they are grumpy. If they have an odd style which works, leave it.

If you know that you are not the source of the problem and that this is not a style issue, it is probably time to have a coaching and feedback discussion with the person who is demotivated. Do not be surprised if it takes several attempts to complete the conversation. When someone is down, they tend not to want to open up about it, especially to the boss. If you ask 'How are you?' they will reply 'OK' which moves you nowhere. Ask the open question 'How are you on a scale of 1 to 10?' and then ask 'How can we move you closer to 10?' or 'What is holding you back from 10?'

You may find work-related reasons behind the demotivation, in which case you are lucky. These reasons can be dealt with. More often you will find personal reasons lurking in the background. This is dangerous territory. You are the boss, not a psychologist or marriage counsellor. Don't mess in areas where your goodwill could do great damage. As a boss you can fix the work side of the problem: give time off, reduce workloads, be supportive. You can also refer the team member to HR for specialist help, if they have that capability.

There is a final possibility. Some people are just very high-maintenance. They always have special needs, they are always in special circumstances, they always need special attention. And it is always 'me me me'. You have a decision to make. Some high-maintenance people are high-performing and you can go along with their antics. But ultimately, they are responsible for their own motivation: they should not put the monkey on your back. You are not there to satisfy every whim they have: you create the conditions in which the team can be motivated and you should support each individual reasonably. But once you start indulging special demands, you find that fulfilling one request simply opens the door to another request. Stand your ground.

How do I set targets and workloads?

Factory work tends to be measurable. You can measure how many cars or burgers or widgets are made each minute, and how many people are required to do the work. You can measure quantity, quality and variances. Office work is different. It is ambiguous and open-ended. You have no objective way of knowing how much is enough.

Perhaps our best guide is the English romantic poet William Blake, who was writing at the start of the Industrial Revolution. In the *Proverbs of Hell* he wrote: 'You never know what is enough unless you know what is more than enough.' You cannot know what your limit is until you have exceeded it.

In practice, this means you should be ambitious in setting goals and workloads for your team. They will let you know when they have more than enough, or when you have asked for the impossible. And keep your eyes and ears open. In Japan the *kacho*, or section head, sits at the head of their section where they can see and hear what everyone is doing. It is then very clear whether the workload is too high or not.

> be ambitious in setting goals and workloads for your team

Within the broad principle of 'more is better', you need to know how to set targets. This is where another common acronym helps. Good targets should be SMART targets, where SMART stands for:

- specific
- measurable

- actionable
- relevant
- time limited.

If you think about it, this is better than the alternative:

- vague
- not measurable
- not actionable
- irrelevant
- with no time limit.

A good example of a SMART target was President John F. Kennedy's announcement that the United States would put a man on the moon and bring him back again within ten years. It ticks all the boxes of a SMART goal. The relevant criteria were met because the moon shot was a direct response to the Soviet Union's launch of Sputnik. The USA could not afford to lose space to its Cold War enemy, and this was the goal that focused the efforts of a nation.

You do not need to tell your team to go to the moon. But a good target for them will be SMART:

- **Specific:** this is what we will achieve.
- **Measurable:** this is how we will know when we have got there.
- **Actionable:** this is what each of us can do to help us all get there.
- **Relevant:** this is why it is important to each of us, to the team and to the firm.
- **Time limited:** this is when we must achieve it by.

If you can set stretching targets in this framework, you will be able to focus and direct the efforts of your team.

How do I delegate well?

Delegation is a core skill which is rarely taught. We are expected to pick it up as we go along. That can be a bruising experience, especially for our team members. Many managers struggle with this basic task.

As ever, the way for you to work out how to delegate is to recall what your best bosses did when they delegated to you. Here is a delegation checklist to help you develop your own best practice:

- If in doubt, delegate. Even if your team is only 60% ready, trust them. They will rise to the challenge if you give them the chance, and they will be grateful to you.

- Don't just delegate the routine rubbish: delegate challenging tasks as well.

- Be clear about your goals; use SMART targets as outlined in the previous section on target setting.

- Check for understanding. You may have explained what you want, but do not assume that means your team understands.

- Set clear expectations about reporting and monitoring.

- Be clear about the goals but flexible about the means. Your team may well come up with a better solution and a better approach. Trust them. They will be committed to a project they own more than to a project that you own and micro-manage, giving them zero discretion.

- You can delegate responsibility, but you cannot delegate accountability. You are still accountable for the outcome, so make sure it is a good outcome.

- Set your team up for success. Make sure they have enough time, budget and support to do what you want them to do.

> if in doubt, delegate;
> don't micro-manage

- Don't micro-manage. If you delegate, delegate. Micro-management is a sign either that you are a control freak or that you do not trust your team. Either way, it is not a good sign. Have the courage to let go.

● Be available to support your team as their manager coach.

Delegation is like a credit card. You set a generous limit to start with and see if each team member is worth their delegation limit. Those who rise to the challenge have justified their delegation credit limit, so you should now raise their limit and delegate more. Others may struggle to pay back your trust in them, and you learn to delegate less to them. This is art, not science. Done well, it is a beautiful art which lets your team flourish and allows you to achieve more and work less.

Who should I hire?

Building the right team is fundamental to your success. Over the years, hiring processes have become ever more sophisticated. 'Sophisticated' in this case means long drawn out, varied, demanding and expensive. Lots of fancy new psychometric tools are rolled out in the hope of sorting out the gems from the garbage. And at the end of it all, we still make mistakes.

So how do you decide? If you are hiring in the marketplace, you will more or less certainly find a raft of candidates with outstanding technical skills and good track records. And they will all strive to make a good impression in interview. So you are left with a dead heat: you may as well ask them to pick straws.

Over the years, only two things have helped me drive my success rate up. First, take references. References are often provided and often not used. Don't rely on what is written: that will have been sanitised by lawyers to avoid saying anything actionable. Talk to the referee. Most mistakes are weeded out very fast.

The second tie breaker is values. Hire to values, not to skills. You can train skills, but you cannot train values. If someone is highly talented but with the wrong values, just walk away.

'Hiring to values' sounds vague and unhelpful. Here is how you can do it. Draw a series of characters, like the Mr Men cartoons of long ago. Your characters may include Mr (or Ms) Grumpy, Dozy, Fib, Idle, Shifty. Draw whatever characters you do not want. Now draw another set of cartoon characters who you would like: Mr (or Ms) Helpful, Energetic, Responsible, Positive. Now get your team to see which sort of characters your candidates are. This cuts through all the complicated psychobabble and reduces the decision to a series of short, sharp contrasts.

This is very, very unsophisticated. Which is probably why it works.

Giving negative feedback: formal assessments

There are a few people who positively enjoy giving bad reviews. These are the bosses who are well worth not working for. Most people hate giving bad reviews. It feels like you are treating a colleague like a child who needs to be scolded. The result is a disaster. The message gets mangled and you have an emotional train wreck on both sides. So in practice, everything gets sugar coated. Typically, 90% of staff are rated as average or above: statistically impossible and emotionally inevitable. And any problems come wrapped in code words such as 'development opportunities' (weaknesses) or 'challenges' (crushing weaknesses).

The first rule of giving assessments is to follow company procedure and stay on the right side of employment law. The law may be daft and company procedures may be insane, but you gain nothing by taking on the law and your company.

Here are the four principles to help you make the most of an awkward situation:

- **No surprises.** If you have been a good coach, there should be no surprises at evaluation time. This requires crystal clear and consistent feedback and discussion throughout the year.

- **Be clear.** If a team member has not been a team player, don't say 'some people complain that you have not helped them enough ...'. This simply opens up an argument. Show what your evaluation is, and be ready to give specific examples of why you think that is a fair evaluation. Keep it short and direct; avoid using weasel words such as might, maybe, perhaps, sometimes .... Don't let there be confusion, because confusion leads to conflict: 'But you said ... and I thought you meant ..., then why didn't you ....'

- **Check for understanding.** This can be painful, but it is important. Before moving on to how your team member can move forward, check for understanding and agreement. You can do this by summarising: 'So I gave you a 3 out of 5 on this criterion: is that fair?' Be ready to back up your view. Make sure you have cleared your view with HR and your boss beforehand, so that if your team member wants to contest your view, you are covered. Hold firm, unless you have made an obvious error of fact.

- **Be positive.** This is where you move from performance ('this is how you have performed') to development ('this is what you can do about it'). Ideally, this should be a coaching discussion, but when you have just delivered bad news your team member may not be in the right frame of mind for coaching. Fix a time when you can move to the positive agenda.

Should I fire a team member?

This is a question most coaches hate having to deal with: you know you are seriously messing with someone's life without full command of the facts. In the same way, many managers hate dealing with this. Especially if you have never fired someone before, this is a traumatic decision. Unfortunately, once managers have tasted blood, quite a few secretly enjoy the power of wielding the axe in the belief that it makes them look strong and will encourage others to fall in line. Between fear and love of wielding the axe, there is the team member whose future you are deciding. How do you go about it?

It is easy to get blinded by emotion. I have found managers wanting to fire team members for highly personal reasons:

- The team member outshines me and hogs the limelight.
- The team member is disrespectful: she walks through doors before me (I cannot make these things up ...).
- The team member embarrassed me in public.
- Top management expect to see heads roll, and I want to make sure it is not mine.
- The team member really irritates me (which means they have different working styles).
- The best way for me to take control is to fire a few people: everyone else will then realise who the boss is. No more nonsense from anyone ....

Start by depersonalising the situation, even though it is highly personal. Do an honest evaluation of the team member's strengths, weaknesses and contribution. Occasionally, the decision is made very easy for you, as when someone has acted illegally. Most of the time, it is less clear cut despite first impressions. On one occasion I was about to fire a junior who got so drunk at a dinner with the CEO of a client that he passed out. The CEO whispered in my ear 'that's OK – we were all young once. And remember, I said you have to put your liver on

> don't rush to judgement

the line to succeed here, so he was just doing what I told him.' And later I found out that the team member was on medicine, which reacted badly to alcohol. Don't rush to judgement.

As you frame your evaluation, get advice and input from others who have seen your team member at work. You will get one of three outcomes:

- They may confirm your suspicions. By consulting, you will have built political and intellectual support for your decision.

- They may provide good support for your team member. At this point you need to ask why you are the only person seeing any problems. If there is a clash of styles and personality, then that is not a cause for dismissal. You have to work out how to make the most of a team member who is not like you.

- Most likely, you will find fog. There will be conflicting opinions: some faint praise and some doubts.

Where there is fog, you need to differentiate between a team member who has hit a bump in the road, and one who is in the vortex of doom. Here is what the difference looks like:

- Bump in the road employee:
  - There have been mess-ups, which the employee recognises.
  - The employee remains positive.
  - The employee is open to coaching, and learns and grows.
- Vortex of doom employee:
  - You have conversations which go 'I said you said and I meant and anyway she said and it wasn't my fault and you don't understand …'.
  - You agree remedial steps which are then half-met not quite on time, and a barrage of excuses follow.
  - You find it was always someone else's fault (often yours). The employee takes no responsibility and does not recognise failings.

> don't look at the snapshot of performance today; look at progress and attitude

In other words, don't look at the snapshot of performance today. Look at progress and attitude. If a team member takes responsibility and makes progress, they have a chance. If they do not take responsibility and do not make progress, then be bold and wield the axe.

Finally, in large organisations you always have the option of trying to sell the weak team member to another department. In some organisations, especially public sector, this can be standard practice. It avoids the pain and potential legal problems of firing someone. But this does not help: the employee is still in the wrong place; the organisation still has a weak employee; you send out a message that you are not serious about performance management; you look weak and you annoy other managers when you send them weak players. If you need to fire someone, fire them.

How do I fire someone?

Employment law has become a bonanza for lawyers and litigious staff. So the simple message is follow legal process. In practice, that means you talk to HR and make sure you follow their process precisely. If you do not have an HR department, consult your lawyers.

Unfortunately, the legal process is a very bad management process. Our politicians, who have never had to run anything, are focused on fairness. They interpret this as putting in place a long legal process to make sure that everything is documented, and that the employee has the chance to appeal. Legally, the result may be fair. In practice, this sets up an adversarial process: a first warning (with the potential to appeal and have union representation) is followed by a second warning and appeal and finally dismissal with the potential for court action to follow.

Anything you say or do could land up in court. If you move someone to a new role, that could be constructive dismissal.

Within the bounds of HR and legal process, there are a few principles to remember:

- **Act fast.** The longer the sorry saga goes on, the more painful it becomes for everyone.

- **Maintain respect.** Keep the process private; don't undermine the team member in public; give them the chance to decide to leave before they are fired. That makes it easier to write a reference for them and it makes it easier for them to maintain their dignity.

- **Be firm, clear and consistent.** Anything you say is liable to be misinterpreted and may be used against you. Have a script and stick to it.

- **Focus on the survivors.** If you have made the right decision, the rest of your team will heave a gentle sigh of relief that you have removed some dead weight. But they will also be anxious about where they stand. This is your chance to set expectations both in private and in public about the way forward: use the opportunity.

Note

10 Queen, *The Miracle*, 1989.

Chapter 7
Dealing with events

When Prime Minister Harold Macmillan was asked by a journalist what might derail his government, he is reputed to have replied: 'events, dear boy, events'.[11] As with Prime Ministers, so with managers. We have our plans, we have our teams and all is going well, at least on paper. And then along come events to spoil our well-laid plans.

For us, events may be unexpected. But the events themselves are predictable. Like having a car accident: to us, it will be completely unexpected and a shock. To our insurance company, it is so predictable that they can make money by insuring us: they know exactly how likely we are to claim, given our profile.

Many of the unexpected events you will face are routine: I can predict that they will happen, although I have no idea if they will happen to you or when they will happen. If we know that

> if you know how to handle crises and events, they can be your chance to shine

something is likely to happen, it makes sense to be ready. Crises will happen: we cannot tell exactly what the crisis will be, but we know from experience of many other crises what good and bad practice looks like. If you know how to handle crises and events, they can be your chance to shine.

Here are some of the more common events which managers raise:

- ethical problems
- managing crises
- how can I influence decisions?
- making decisions in uncertainty
- how do I deal with this project successfully?
- presentation phobia
- how do I network?

Ethical problems

Ethics is where theory and practice part company. Organisations make great play of how ethical they are. And then you start to realise there are places where you prefer not to look too closely at who is doing what and how they are doing it. Ignorance seems to be bliss.

Ethical problems come in two main flavours:

- Do I blow the whistle when I see malpractice?
- How far do I go in bending the rules?

Many firms encourage you to speak up if you see malpractice. As ever, watch the feet and not the mouth. Your firm may say it encourages whistle blowers, but look at what happens when someone does blow the whistle. The standard reaction of many organisations is first to cover up the problem and then shoot the whistle blower. If you are lucky, you will be fired with a pot of gold linked to a confidentiality clause. The firm does not want to be embarrassed, so they want to shut you up with the pot of gold. And they do not want a troublemaker, so they will fire you.

And then it gets worse. Whistle blowing tends to be high profile. You will quickly be known as a whistle blower in your industry and possibly beyond. That means you will mysteriously find doors being shut in your face when you look for employment elsewhere. Employers value loyalty highly, and whistle blowing is the ultimate act of treachery. No one wants to hire a traitor and troublemaker, even if they are talented.

If you have good ethics, you should speak up. If you want to stay in your job, you should learn Admiral Lord Nelson's trick: use your blind eye to look at things you do not want to see.

As ever, prevention is better than cure. Remember the dictum of legendary investor Warren Buffett: 'When a management with a reputation for brilliance tackles a business with a reputation for poor fundamental economics, it is the reputation of the business that remains intact.' We all tend to rise or fall to the standards around us. We succumb to groupthink, which is how scandals emerge, as we have all seen in politics and banking over the last few years.

Different industries have different profiles for ethics, corruption, fair trading and ecological responsibility. My lawyers advise me not to name names, but we all know who the prime suspects are in each case. If you join a firm with a lousy reputation, that is the reputation you will have to live with.

If you find yourself in a firm with 'flexible' ethics, it is hard to keep to the moral high ground. You have to either sign up or sign out. If you sign up, you are unlikely to find yourself handing over envelopes of cash to the local minister of procurement. It is rarely so black and white. You may hire a local agent, distributor or fixer who does all the dirty work for you, while you look the other way. You can pretend your hands are clean.

Ultimately, you have to ask yourself two questions about what you are doing:

- Would I feel comfortable telling my parents/children about this?
- How would this look in court and on the front page of a newspaper?

If you are not happy with the answers, you are probably doing the wrong thing and may be in the wrong place.

None of this is encouraging for a high-ethics person who is surrounded by poor ethics. Plan your career to work in an industry and a firm which meets your ethical standards.

Managing crises

Crises make and break managers. Look at them positively: this is your chance to shine, to learn, to grow, to become more resilient – which may or may not help when the crisis first appears. So how should you react?

> crises make and break managers: look at them positively

Think about what you have learned from how colleagues or bosses have handled crises. What are the do's and don'ts that you have observed? Start with the negative lessons: this will tell you what *not* to do. Typically, the negative lessons include:

- Hide the problem and act too late. Crises do not solve themselves; they tend to get worse, not better over time.
- Start an inquest: you cannot move forwards by looking backwards.
- Start the blame game: watch the politics erupt and no action will happen.

You can add to the list of don'ts. Now turn it around. How have some of your role models handled crises well? Some of the typical answers include:

- **Stay calm and positive.** Wear the mask of leadership. Even if you feel bad inside, do not share your fears. Your little cloud of gloom will spread like an evil depression across the team. Create a sense of hope and possibility.

- **Drive to action.** Create a sense of momentum. Curiously, even if you have to change direction you will be forgiven. Everyone wants a solution, and if you are seen to be moving to a solution, others will follow.

- **Act early.** The sooner you act, the more likely you are to keep things under control.

- **Get help.** Don't be a lone super-hero: they only succeed in the movies. In an organisation, teams work. Build your coalition of support. Make sure your boss and your boss's boss know what is going on and support you. This takes time and effort, but no one said management is easy.

- **Overcommunicate.** There will be fear, uncertainty and doubt. The rumour mill will be working overtime. Make sure that your script is the one which everyone follows.

Long after the crisis is over, everyone will forget exactly what you did. But they will remember very clearly how you behaved, even if they cannot pin you down on the specifics. Make sure you behave the way you want to be remembered.

> long after the crisis is over, everyone … will remember very clearly how you behaved

How can I influence decisions?

The nature of work today is for managers to find that their responsibility exceeds their authority. This is uncomfortable. We depend on people and forces that are beyond our control. We may not control them, but we are still responsible. We still have to influence events in our favour.

Perhaps the most important decision we have to influence is our budget. If you agree to a 'challenging' budget which top management proposes, you will have two weeks of basking in the warm glow of appreciation. You will look very macho. You will then have 50 weeks of stress trying to meet your macho budget. Meanwhile, a colleague who negotiated a better budget will have an easier time and will get a bonus at year-end for beating their budget. So how do you influence a budget or any other decision which is beyond your control?

Fortunately, this is an area where research and experience point the same way. Daniel Kahneman won the Nobel Prize for Economics in 2002, and much of his work has been on decision-making heuristics: the short cuts people use to make decisions. You can use these to your advantage. Here are the main decision-making heuristics:

● **Anchoring.** Is the moon more or less than two million miles from Earth? I have no idea. But I have just anchored the debate around two million. It could be one million or ten million. You anchor a decision by following the method of the Welsh rugby team in the 1980s: get your retaliation in first. Be the first to act. State your position and let others work around it.

● **Repetition.** All good dictators and advertisers have long known that the more you say something, the more likely people are to believe it. Keep pushing the same simple message time and time again: eventually it will become the received wisdom unless someone else has the time and stamina to keep on challenging you. For most people, it is too much effort and too much risk to pick battles which are not strictly necessary.

● **Social proof.** If Usain Bolt wears those shoes, then maybe I will run faster if I buy the same shoes. Some hope! But the power of endorsement is strong. You will not get Usain Bolt to endorse your budget proposal and you do not need him: you need endorsement from a few key power players. Know who they are and bring them onside early. Once they are on board, let everyone know: build the bandwagon effect. No one wants to be left out of a success.

- **Framing.** Do you want to spend another $5 million on marketing? Probably not. Would you like to invest $5 million to protect our market share, stop the competition and keep the factories running at full capacity to maximise our profits? Probably yes. They are, of course, the same decision framed differently. Pitch your proposal the right way. Make it easy for people to say 'yes'.

- **Restricted choice.** We have 317 ways of launching this product: which is best? Most people will give up. And if anyone is brave enough to choose, they will immediately regret their choice: they will always suspect that one of the other 316 ways might have been better. Instead, you are now asked to launch the product in one of three ways:
  - The very expensive and fancy way which could do very well.
  - The very cheap way which will not get much in the way of results but will avoid too many losses.
  - The middle way which is affordable and will still get great results.

Most people will pick the choice you meant them to pick: the middle way. If you give a choice, make it simple. And make sure they make the right choice.

- **Emotional relevance.** If competition is getting stronger then so what? That is dull analysis, even if I am told it threatens jobs. If the competition is getting stronger and a few colleagues are made redundant, then clearly things are serious. If my job is now on the line, it is time to press the panic button. You need to make a business case for change or decisions: you also need to make a personal case. Show what will happen if you do not get your way (personal disaster) and if you do get your way (personal success).

- **Loss aversion.** Let's toss a coin. If I win, you give me $1 million. If I lose, I give you $1.1 million. Rationally, this is a good bet for you. Do it enough times and you will become rich. But back on planet Earth, few people would take that risk. The prospect of losing $1 million offsets any potential gain. In the office, loss aversion is not about losing money: that is part of doing business. The real risk is that you are made to look foolish in front of your peers. People will go to great lengths to keep face. So keep all your disagreements in private, but publicise all your agreements fast.

> you need endorsement from a few key power players: know who they are and bring them onside early

Perhaps the most important lesson is that you can and should influence any decisions which affect you. Too many managers trust the organisation and trust the process. Don't trust the process: work the process in your favour.

Making decisions in uncertainty

The good news is that management is full of ambiguity, uncertainty and confusion. That is good, because it means there will always be the need for management. We will not be replaced by computers any time soon. The even better news is that these tough situations let good managers stand out.

So how do you make a decision in uncertainty?

The most radical solution I heard from a client was simple: toss a coin. If the decision is really so evenly balanced, then it should not matter which way you go, as long as you decide to go one way or the other. The fatal flaw with this approach is that it ignores reality on the ground: you need to make a decision which the organisation supports. Tossing a coin is not a good basis for building a coalition of support for a billion-dollar investment.

Equally, this gives a clue to how you should make your decision. There is no such thing as a good idea or decision which never happened. You only know if a decision is good if it happens in practice: it needs the support of the organisation. With that in mind, it is easier to make a decision.

Apply a series of screens to your decision:

- What would I recommend if the CEO put me on the spot right now, and did not allow the option of 'more research, analysis and committee meetings'? You are a manager, so manage. You have experience and expertise and you have judgement. Back yourself.

- What would my boss (and the CEO) back? This sounds like weak-willed politics. It is not. It is about finding a solution which will lead to action. If your boss and CEO will not support a decision, it will not happen.

- What will my team back? If your team is very enthusiastic about Option A, back them. Even if it is less than ideal, they will own it and they will want to make it happen. If you inflict on them your choice of Option B, which they do not like, you will find every small problem becomes a mountain to climb.

- What will other stakeholders support? You need to build a coalition of the willing. It is possible that they are all wrong and you should take them on. That sort of fight can accelerate your career: you succeed fast or fail fast.

- Which option is most in line with our strategy and values? You have to be able to argue your case. The strategy and values of the organisation give you the basis on which to make your case.

- What are the financial benefits of each option? In practice, the financial case normally is tweaked to back whatever option you all prefer. If you all prefer Option A, then the financial case for it will be made to look good, while the case for Option B will be made to look bad. The financial case normally provides ammunition to support your view, rather than insight to decide your view. You can tweak assumptions and inputs to suit your case.

All of this is far removed from the logic of business schools, which focus on Bayesian Analysis and Net Present Values. As a practising manager you have to deal with reality.

Remember, you will not find the perfect solution because it does not exist. Most of the time managers have to find the lesser of two evils or the better of two goods. The only good decision is one that happens.

How do I deal with this project successfully?

This question comes in several flavours during coaching sessions. It can also come as:

- 'Help, I am blocked on a project.'
- 'How do I set my project up for success?'

Normally, the best way of tackling this question is to look at how you set a project up for success. If the project is going wrong, it is also worth looking back and seeing if you were set up for success from the start. The blockages you face today are likely to be caused by how you were set up from the start. It pays to deal with causes, not symptoms. Even better, it pays to avoid the problem in the first place by setting yourself up for success.

Here are four questions you need to answer when you set a project up:

- Am I working on the right problem?
- Have I got the right sponsor?
- Have I got the right team and resources?
- Have I got the right approach?

Let's look at each question in turn.

Am I working on the right problem?

This is a two-part question. First, is this right for you in terms of your career and what you like doing? A good project will let you build your career skills and find a claim to fame, and you will enjoy it. A bad project is one you do not enjoy, you build no skills and you gain no recognition.

> the right problem is one which has visibility and relevance two levels above you

Second, the right problem is one which has visibility and relevance two levels above you. It is hopefully both urgent and important. High-stakes projects allow you to accelerate your career: you will succeed fast or you will fail fast.

You want visibility and relevance for your project because these are the projects which will get management support: you will be able to negotiate for the right team, right resources and right support. Lesser projects attract less support and mean that you will work with the B team, not the A team.

An early test of the problem is to ask 'What benefits will come from this?' If you are met with mush such as 'we will all be more dynamic and empowered, have higher self-esteem and customer attitudes will improve', quietly walk away. These are worthy but not compelling goals. The real support goes behind projects which have a strong financial payoff, because managers know that they are worth investing in. This means you should size the prize:

> the real support goes behind projects which have a strong financial payoff

put a monetary value on success. Improving time to market, raising quality and increasing market share are all non-financial benefits: with minimal effort you can show the financial implications of achieving these goals.

Have I got the right sponsor?

Put simply, projects for the CEO never fail. At least, no one will admit that they have failed and huge effort will be put into making them succeed. You will get the backing of the whole organisation and nobody will be too keen to put obstacles in your way. On the other hand, a project for the Head of Stationery to improve utilisation of photocopier paper may be worthy, but will not get the sort of backing you really need.

The right sponsor may not do much, but what they do is vital. They should get the project started by setting the goal and agreeing the team and resources, and they will come in at the end to declare victory. But they are also crucial when you hit a road block. They will normally have the access, power and resources to unblock the way for you in a few minutes, potentially saving you weeks of wasted time. When managers fret that they are facing road blocks which they cannot move, often the root cause is the lack of a strong sponsor. Get this right from the start.

Have I got the right team and resources?

As always, make sure you have the A team working with you. They will succeed where the B team will struggle. Do not simply accept what the assignment process throws at you. HR is normally under pressure to place staff who are under-used. They are under-used for good reason: either they are untried or they have not covered themselves in glory in the past. This is not the team that will work magic for you.

> target the people you want to work with

You need to be your own head hunter. Target the people you want to work with. Talk to them. Flatter them. Take time to understand them: play on their hopes and fears. By doing all of this, you will make them feel wanted. They will start to look at you as the great boss they have never had. They will suddenly and mysteriously become available for you.

If necessary, lean on your sponsor to make sure you get the right team. This is a good test of your sponsor. If they cannot get the right team for you, they probably do not have the power you need to support you. You may want to walk away.

This is also the moment to make sure your two other resources are in place: time and money. Ask for too much of both. You will be bargained down, and you will find your project takes longer and costs more than you first estimated. You need a cushion.

Have I got the right approach?

This is where professional project managers get very excited about critical paths, GANTT charts, risk logs, issue logs and the whole paraphernalia of project management. The reality is, however, that if you have the right team, right resources, right sponsor and right problem, the approach will sort itself out. If nothing else, you can get a good project manager onto the team to do formal project management for you. But you may not want to do this: they can make things very complicated and slow you down. Unless your project is very large and complicated, you will not need formal project management tools: the PRINCE 2 qualification with its 31 key activities and seven work processes is a dead weight, not an enabler, for most projects.

Here is how you can make sure you have the right approach:

- **Start at the end.** 'First things first' is nonsense: that leads to a random walk from the present to the future. Be clear about your goals and focus on them.
- **Work from the back.** Work out the minimum number of steps and activities required to reach your goal. Be clear about dependencies: what has to happen before something else can start. You can always make it complicated later: start with a simple map of how to get from where you are to the finish line.
- **Break it down into simple steps.** Take each step and activity and break it down into a series of simple, bite-sized

chunks. Make sure each activity has an owner who knows what they need to deliver and when they need to deliver it.

- **Identify potential road blocks and issues now.** Start working to remove them now: don't wait until it becomes a crisis.

- **Put in place simple governance, and stick to it.** This allows you to know when things are on track, it gives prompt notice of when you need to take remedial action, and it provides a vehicle for raising issues and keeping your bosses up-to-date. It may feel like boring routine, but it is vital.

Presentation phobia

If you are worried about making a presentation, then you are not alone. Even the best presenters feel nervous before a presentation. Some nerves mean that the adrenalin is running and you are taking the presentation seriously. Someone who feels no nerves and simply stands on stage to read a script will probably bore the audience to tears.

Presentation phobia normally comes down to four fears:

- I do not have the skill.
- I am going to look foolish.
- I do not know what to say.
- I do not know how to say it.

Let's deal with each in turn.

I do not have the skill

Very few executives are skilled presenters. Listening to the average presentation at a business meeting is a good cure for insomnia. So you are not there to entertain. You are there because you have something to offer: you have information, expertise, a point of view, a recommendation which others want to hear. Your task is to communicate your idea or knowledge as simply and as clearly as possible. If you do that, you will be doing far better than most business presenters. You may not be an expert presenter, but you are expert in your area. You have something to contribute. Focus on that.

> communicate your idea or knowledge as simply and as clearly as possible

I am going to look foolish

Everyone worries about looking foolish in front of their peers. The best way to succeed is to rehearse. And then rehearse again. And again. Ask your long-suffering family to suffer a bit more; ask a trusted colleague to help you out; embarrass yourself in front of a mirror. Get all your mistakes out of the way in private. Get feedback on what works and what does not work and build your confidence.

And if you can, check out where you will be presenting beforehand. Use the excuse of familiarising yourself with the technology and logistics, which you need to do anyway. The more comfortable you are with the surroundings, the more confident you will feel. Once you are familiar with the meeting room, visualise success. Imagine your presentation goes well: what it sounds like, looks like, feels like. And then go and do it. Visualising

> imagine your presentation goes well

success is one of the tricks of great performers in sports and arts. Finally, ask a trusted colleague to do a visual check of you before you start. Make sure you are not having a hair or dress disaster.

I do not know what to say

You are the expert, so you should know your topic. Pulling it together is harder. Here are the principles:

- **Tell a story.** This has three parts:
  - This is where we are: introduce the topic, why it is relevant, and your agenda.
  - This is where we are going (recommendation or insight).
  - This is how we get there (how it works).

- **Focus your story.** In a large group, there is probably only one person you really need to persuade or influence. Focus your story on that person. This will ensure:
  - You will keep the presentation short and simple.
  - You will be focused and interesting. Look at the world through the eyes of the person you need to influence: what do they need to hear; what will they ask?

- **Reduce, reduce, reduce.** A presentation is like a diamond: it benefits from good cutting.
  - Short sentences and short words work.
  - No more than 20 words per slide: you want a smart presenter and dumb slides, not a dumb presenter with smart slides. Don't read your slides: use them so that all they do is show where you are in your presentation.

- **Support assertions with facts.**
  - Don't make claims you cannot support. And check your facts: one bad fact can destroy a presentation.

- **Make it active.**
  - Use active verbs; avoid the passive tense, which may sound grand but is boring.
  - Use real stories of real people: stories engage. Relate dry facts to real examples. Bring it to life.

By now, you should know what to say, you should realise that you are the expert with the skill, and you should have removed most of the fear of looking foolish, through preparation and rehearsal. But still people worry that they do not have presentation skills: *how* do you present?

I do not know how to say it

Try this exercise. Explain the tax implications of the transfer pricing system in your organisation. If you fall asleep before your colleagues do, you have failed. Now tell your colleagues about the most exciting (legal and decent) thing you have done in the last year. The chances are that you will come to life, and your colleagues may even wake up. You will have shown that you have all the skills needed to present well: you will have shown energy, enthusiasm and expertise.

> your presentation will be remembered … for one big fact and for what you were like

Now try a second exercise. Try to remember a presentation from over six months ago. It will be hard to remember much about it. You will remember two things at most:

- one big message or fact
- what the presenter was like.

And this is how your presentation will be remembered. It will be remembered for one big fact and for what you were like. So what is the one big idea you want your presentation to be remembered for? Organise your presentation around that one idea. Second, how do you want to be remembered? As a dull mumbler, or as someone with energy, excitement and enthusiasm?

Energy, excitement and enthusiasm are the magic three E's of presenting. The best way to achieve these three E's is to permit yourself to enjoy your presentation. You are the expert; you are allowed to enjoy showing off your knowledge. If you are not enthusiastic, no one else will be enthusiastic for you. Go for it.

> energy, excitement and enthusiasm are the magic three E's of presenting

How do I network?

Some people gain huge energy and enjoyment from being thrust into a room full of strangers with the chance to meet new people and make new contacts. For many others, such events are full of dread: having to make small talk to strangers you do not want to meet and will probably never meet again. Neither of these approaches is much good from a business perspective. Networking is not a random event: it should have a purpose. Know why you are networking and set yourself a goal.

There are two sorts of networking: planned and opportunistic. Opportunistic networking is where you go to a big event and hope to meet some useful people. Planned networking is where you target key individuals and find ways of meeting them.

We will deal with each one separately.

Opportunistic networking: the big networking event and conferences

Look carefully at who speaks to whom at big conferences. For the most part people are not extending their networks: they are reinforcing existing networks. Look at what happens at your company conference: it will be tribal. Bosses talk to other bosses; the Paris office talks to the Paris office; HR people talk to HR people. This is not all bad. These are the people you need to work with most on a day-to-day basis, and it makes sense to strengthen your links with them. But it is also an opportunity missed. The same sort of thing happens at public conferences: people gravitate to people they already know.

If you go to one of these events, plan ahead. Find out who is going and work through the delegate list. There are probably a few people you either need or want to meet. Target them. Do some homework on them so you have something to talk about together: find something you can compliment them about. Find their photograph so that at least you know what they look like. Google and social media are wonderful tools – use them.

At the event, success is not measured in the number of business cards you collect. It is measured in meeting people you need to meet.

> success ... is measured in meeting people you need to meet

Perhaps the hardest step is the introduction. Saying 'hello, I'm Jim from finance' will lead to an awkward silence while the other person looks over your shoulder in the desperate hope they can spot someone else they want to talk to.

The best way to get an introduction is to be introduced: normally there will be someone who knows both you and your target. Ask them to effect the introduction. Otherwise, introduce yourself with a suitable ice breaker. Flattery always works. For instance, you can follow up 'hello, I'm Jim from finance' with:

- 'I read that wonderful article of yours ...'
- 'I enjoyed your speech on ...'
- 'I hear you are doing great work on ...'

This then lets you explain why you are interested in talking to them. Then follow up with a question. People will always talk about their favourite subject: themselves. So ask them more about their work. Normally, there is no need to make your great pitch there and then. Make contact and agree to follow up later, when you can have a proper discussion about your mutual interest.

Planned networking

The other main form of networking is planned. This is strategic networking where you target key individuals. It will take time: it is an investment in building your network, gaining access and growing your influence. First, work out who you need in your network:

- Who do you need in your network to make things happen? Who needs to help you?
- Who are the useful sources of information that you need onside?
- Who are the decision makers who can make or break initiatives?
- Who are the influencers whose advice carries weight? Some may be informal advisers, others may have formal roles in finance, marketing, HR or IT where their advice will be sought on any new idea.
- Who are the gatekeepers who can either block or open access to key executives for you?

Draw up an organisation chart with all these people on it, then see how well established you are with each one. A few questions will help keep your assessment honest:

- When did I last speak to them?
- Were they helpful, hostile or neutral?
- Do I understand their personal and professional agendas?
- When am I due to speak with them again?

If you do not know the answers to these questions, assume you do not have a good relationship. You need to do your networking.

Networking is particularly important if you are working on a project where you will need support from these people. Don't leave it too late. Introduce yourself early and ask for their advice. This is the coach manager's way of influencing.

Don't sell to them and make a big pitch. Involve them early. By asking them for their advice they will feel flattered and involved. If they raise any killer issues, you have time to work on them.

Even if they do not raise killer issues, you will be able to go back to them later and show how your idea or project now incorporates their advice. The chances are that you are doing what you would have done anyway, but give them credit for coming up with

> involve them early: by asking them for their advice they will feel flattered and involved

their insights. People rarely oppose their own ideas, so make the idea theirs.

Finally, understand the role of social media. Social media are very good at helping you find out about people. But there is no point in having a thousand contacts on LinkedIn and Facebook if no one will actually return your call. There is a vast difference between a contact on social media and a personal relationship. A good network is deep, not broad: it will be full of people you can call on for help and advice. These relationships are not built by Twitter. They are built by meeting people face to face: invest time and effort in your network. Go for depth, not breadth, of relationships.

Note

11 This quotation is contested. It has passed into folklore and is certainly in the style of Macmillan, although some argue he never actually said it.

Chapter 8

Coaching and working with colleagues

The art of management is making things happen through people we do not control. This is not easy. We are meant to collaborate with our fiercest rivals. Your real competition is not a rival firm: it is sitting at a desk near you. Your colleagues are competing with you for the same pot of promotions, budget, bonuses, and management time and attention. They have different priorities and needs, which they will push at your expense. Then we wonder why there is tension in the office.

We can choose our friends, but we can not choose our colleagues. We have to work with them, whatever our personal feelings may be. Basic professional etiquette enables us to get along, and defines the rules of engagement in our organisation. But beneath the veneer of

> politics is a reality of office life, even if we pretend that it does not exist

cooperation, there will always be competition, which can get ugly. Politics is a reality of office life, even if we pretend that it does not exist.

Issues with colleagues can be complicated, messy and emotional. There is rarely a right or wrong answer. Here are some of the more common issues you are likely to face:

- How do I work with people I do not like or trust?
- Dealing with bullies and other awkward people
- Dealing with conflict between departments and groups

- When should I fight?
- Dealing with rumour and innuendo
- What do I do about consultants?
- How do I tell someone they annoy me?

How do I work with people I do not like or trust?

This question gets emotional and messy fast. There is always a history in which the other person is the complete villain. But a good manager coach has to be objective, learning to see things from both sides. The goal is not to pass judgement: you do not need to prove who is wrong or right. The goal is understanding. You need to understand what is happening before you can do much about it.

> the goal is not to pass judgement ... the goal is understanding

You do not need to like people in order to work with them. But you do need respect and trust. So your starting point is to disentangle liking from trust and respect. Be specific: lack of trust comes from three things:

- Lack of familiarity: I simply don't know enough about this person. This heals itself over time.
- They don't do what they say: I cannot rely on their word. Be careful here: you may have said one thing and they may have heard another thing.
- They say one thing to my face and another thing behind my back. Agreements last as long as we are in the same room. Again, be careful: they may have their version of this story. If this sort of dispute goes public, mud will stick to both of you.

We will deal with people you don't trust and people you don't like separately.

Dealing with lack of trust

The chances are that lack of trust is mutual. You may see this as completely unreasonable because you know you can trust yourself. Put that to one side. Arguing about who can and cannot be trusted simply leads to less trust on both sides.

Building trust takes time. If you have a trust issue, you need to deal with it explicitly. You cannot hope it will just go away. You have three ways of dealing with this.

First, be brave and find a good time to talk to the person you cannot trust in private. Your goal is not to confront but to find a solution to a problem. The tone of the meeting should be collaborative. Start by laying out the challenge in a non-confrontational way: 'We have had our misunderstandings, and I fear that is stopping us working as well together as we should: what could we do to work better?' Avoid going over history. Focus on the way forward.

> avoid going over history: focus on the way forward

This discussion can land up in a general statement of goodwill, which does not do very much for either of you. Find specific actions that you both need to take on current projects which will show you can both deliver to each other. Agree to put these next steps in emails to each other so that there is no confusion about what was really meant.

When the other side delivers, make sure you recognise them. Thank them and copy their boss on the email. Like training a toddler with tantrums, you need to reinforce good behaviour whenever you can.

Each time they fail to deliver on their side of the bargain, have another discussion with them. If this does not work and leads to more argument, you need a Plan B.

The alternative way of dealing with lack of trust is to work around the person you do not trust. Reduce or eliminate dependence on that person, if you can. If neither of these ways works, and your work depends on the person you trust, you have to go to Plan C.

Plan C requires the support of your boss. You do not want to involve your boss in resolving an interpersonal issue of trust: your boss cannot do that and will not thank you for asking. You have to present both the problem and the solution. Be clear that there is a lack of trust and that it threatens progress on your unit's goals. Forget about trying to forge a great relationship. Focus on the transactions which have to happen. Have clear and open discussions with the colleague you do not trust: don't try to negotiate by email. But then put every oral agreement and request into an email to confirm it, and copy to your boss. If there are any issues, such as impossible demands, you can then deal with them as they arise on a purely transactional basis. This is painful and low trust and your boss will not like it. But if it is the only way of making progress, do it.

Dealing with people you do not like

Compared to working with people you don't trust, this is relatively easy as long as you trust them. Remember, trust means that you can rely on their word. If you can rely on someone, you don't need to like them.

If you don't like someone, the chances are that the feelings are mutual. You may show your dislike unwittingly in your body language, the way you talk and the way you behave. You may mean well, but your thoughts will betray you. A quick test: when did you last thank or praise the person you don't like? When did you show them respect and flatter them by asking for their advice? If you thank, praise, ask and flatter, you can quickly change perceptions.

Behind most personal clashes are style differences. For instance, this is how A might see B:

A sees self as ...	A sees B as ...
I am good with people.	Why can't B get out of his dull reports and deal with people properly?
I see the big picture and understand what is important.	Why does B keep on nitpicking about irrelevant detail and slow us all down?
I am flexible and creative in making things happen.	B is a control freak and neatness freak who is obsessed with processes and procedures, so nothing ever actually happens.

Now turn this around. This is B's view of the world:

B sees self as ...	B sees A as ...
I am strong on reality: I deal with facts, not opinions.	A spends her whole time politicking and gossiping to gain favour and advance her career.
I stay on top of the operation and make sure things don't go wrong.	A is full of airy-fairy ideas and could not run a bath, let alone a business.
If anyone can get us from X to Y, it is me.	A is a complete mess, totally disorganised.

There is no point in debating who is right or wrong. Both are different. If they could learn to work together they would make a great team: they have complementary strengths.

This is your task: to work out how you can adapt your style to that of the person you don't like. Make an effort to get in tune with them. Put yourself in the shoes of A and work out how you could adapt. It might be something like this:

> adapt your style to that of the person you don't like

Next time I meet I will ask him for his views on the topic we're discussing. I will not roll my eyes in disgust or boredom when he plies me with facts, figures and details. I will try to learn something. I will encourage him to look after the detail, and in return I will work the politics and people: he will like me taking that problem away from him. I will let him take control of how to make it happen, which saves me effort and which he will enjoy.

Occasionally, you will find that there is no work style difference: you simply do not like the person. You dislike their hair, their teeth, their dress, their jokes, their views about life and society. Tough. That is your problem, not theirs. Unless it is stopping you doing your work, do not raise personal issues. In these circumstances, learn to wear the mask of leadership: be a role model in terms of good behaviour. Leave your personal views in the car park.

In summary, to work with someone you don't like:

- Thank, praise, ask and flatter them.
- Adjust your style to theirs: put your differences to good use.
- Wear the mask of professionalism: leave your personal views outside.

You may never get to like these people, but hopefully you will get to respect each other.

Dealing with bullies and other awkward people

War, famine, pestilence and bullies should not exist in an ideal world, but we don't live in an ideal world. Bullies exist and we have to deal with them. In the world of work, we may not be able to walk away from them.

Bullies typically have three lines of attack:

- Demeaning: 'that is the worst piece of work I have ever seen ....'
- Accusing: 'You clearly don't care ... you never make an effort ... no one can rely on you.'
- Threatening: 'If you don't ... then the sky will fall down.'

This gets very personal very fast, but is always wrapped up in high-minded language around doing what is best for the organisation.

The details of who said what when are not relevant. What counts is how you behave, because that is how you will be remembered by others. And if you behave the right way, the bully will go elsewhere and find easier victims. Assume you have to deal with it yourself. Do not escalate it: you are not a child running to your parents to ask them to stop the playground bully. You are the adult: deal with it.

Here are the three classic ways of dealing with a bully:

- aggressive
- assertive
- passive.

Aggressive reaction does not help. That is like fighting fire with fuel: good if you are a spectator, not so good if you are in the fire. Passive behaviour also does not work: you become the victim and you make the bully very happy. The bullying will just get worse. Focus on assertive behaviour.

Here is what the three sorts of behaviour look like:

Aggressive	Assertive	Passive
I win, you lose	Win–win	Poor me, pity me
Telling: 'You must, I expect'	Negotiating	Pleading: 'Why me?'
Wants to humiliate	Wants a way forward	Wants to avoid conflict
Generalisations: 'That is terrible'	Specifics: 'What is terrible?'	Feelings: 'I feel terrible'
Talks first and loudest	Asks rather than tells; keeps it short and focused	Lets others do the talking
Stares and glares	Appropriate eye contact	Avoids eye contact

Aggressive	Assertive	Passive
Raises voice	Even voice	Quiet voice
Takes a position: 'I must have a 20% discount now'	Looks for common interests: 'How can we reduce your lifetime costs?'	Abandons the position: 'I will ask my boss what discount we can do'
Makes it personal	Focuses on the business	Takes it personally
Needs to control outcome and process	Focuses on the good outcome	Is a victim of events

Effective assertive behaviour in front of a bully will do the following:

- Focus on the outcome, rather than get caught in the process. Don't look back or get sucked into the blame game of what went wrong. Focus on where you need to get to. The bully may take an unreasonable position: find the interest behind the position. A position says 'I want a big discount now'; the interest is 'I want to minimise the lifecycle costs of this product' or 'I need to show my boss I got a good deal'. You are more likely to find common ground on an interest than on a position.

> as soon as you reply to a personal attack with your own personal attack, you will lose

- Avoid self-justification or getting personal. As soon as you reply to a personal attack with your own personal attack, you will lose. The bully will trumpet what you said and hold it up to show how unreasonable you are. The playground reply of 'he started it first' gets you nowhere.

- Deal with the issue, not the personality. That means drive to specifics. If the bully says 'this proposal will be a disaster', don't argue. Ask why, and what the consequences will be. The bully may have a case, which you will have to deal with. They may be bluffing, in which case they will get even more angry. Hold your ground and get clarification.

- Remain calm, positive and reasonable. Act the way you want to be remembered. Don't raise your voice or roll your eyes. Keep to the point. The longer you talk, the more can go wrong. Don't give ammunition to the bully.

All of this is very hard to do in the heat of battle. People who have worked in customer service get plenty of experience in dealing with unpleasant people: working at a hotel or McDonald's as a teenager is very good preparation for management in later life.

Dealing with conflict between departments and groups

Let's assume that another department is not cooperating with you. And also let's assume that you have no way of succeeding without their support. They are quietly undermining you and working to a different agenda. Their behaviour is completely unreasonable and they seem to be impervious to reason. You are starting to take it personally. And the stakes are getting higher all the time: you have deadlines and project goals and budgets to meet. What can you do?

Start by taking the personal poison out of it. All organisations are set up for conflict, whatever the management gurus may claim. Every department has a different window on reality and different priorities; every department is competing for the same limited pot of budget, promotions, and management time and attention. Other departments will cooperate with you because it is in their interests to do so, not because they are kind-hearted.

Churchill said that Russia was 'a riddle, wrapped in a mystery, inside an enigma; but perhaps there is a key. That key is Russian national interest.'[12] The key to unwrapping the mystery of the problem department usually lies with their self-interest. It is quite possible that it is not in their self-interest to do anything more than the absolute minimum to help you: enough to keep top management off their backs.

Your goal is not to prove that they are being unreasonable; it is not to give yourself a defence if things go wrong later; it is not about creating an email trail which you hope will paint you in a good light. Your goal is to make things happen, so you need a range of strategies to secure cooperation.

> your goal is to make things happen, so you need a range of strategies to secure cooperation

At some point you may have to delegate the problem up the hierarchy: ask your boss to step in and sort things out for you. Or perhaps your boss's boss will have to get involved. This may be necessary, but it is not desirable. It shows that you cannot cope: you may or may not have righteousness on your side. All that top management will really understand is that they had to sort out a mess and everyone was pointing fingers at each other. You don't want to go there unless you have to.

The first step is to understand the other department's self-interest. You will not do that by firing off carefully crafted emails or calling for big summit meetings. You will discover their self-interest by talking to them, which in practice means listening to them. You will not find out what is really on their minds in a public meeting: in public they will defend themselves, not open themselves up. A public meeting is one where more than two people are present.

So your first line of defence is to talk to the boss of the problem unit in private. Ideally, catch him or her in the canteen. If you talk informally on neutral territory, you increase your chances of having a sensible conversation. When you talk, you don't have to place your demands on the table right away. Flatter them: thank them for some wonderful support they have given in the past; compliment them on some other work they are doing. Most people feel the need to reciprocate: tit-for-tat can be positive as well as negative. You want the mood of the meeting to be cooperation and support, not conflict. Your colleague will know why you are there, and will normally be relieved that you have not immediately descended into arm wrestling.

Once you have the right mood music, you can lay out your problem and then enquire about their position. Good questions to ask are:

● 'Where does this lie in your priorities?'
● 'What is preventing this getting your support?'

And then listen. Do not argue: they will simply go defensive when you need cooperation, not opposition from them. Recognise that they have a valid point, and then ask if anything else is getting in the way. Once you have a list of their problems, you can ask: 'So if we were able to make those problems go away, would we be able to work together on this?'

This now sets up a problem-solving session where you can help work through their issues. It may well be that they simply have other priorities, in which case you need to understand what would make yours a higher priority from their perspective. If they say something like 'we would need direction from senior management', they have opened the way for you to approach top management with their consent.

So your first strategy is to work collaboratively: find out what is stopping them helping you and solve those problems together.

If you are wise, you will keep your own boss up-to-date. Show that you are having some difficulty, but that you have a plan to sort it out. Keep your boss briefed and up-to-date. Bosses hate surprises.

If the collaborative approach does not work, you need to escalate. You may want to ask for a formal meeting between your department and theirs. The most likely outcome is that the other group will find a way of doing the absolute minimum to avoid being embarrassed in public. You will have minimal compliance, but you will not have true support. Alternatively, you escalate through your boss. You should have kept the boss informed, so it may not be a huge surprise when you ask for his or her advice. If the boss is smart, you will be coached into finding a solution which you will be responsible for. That is not a bad outcome. If the boss is in a good mood, you may find the problem taken away from you. But you will not have covered yourself in glory.

When should I fight?

There are times when you have to stand your ground. You try everything. You try influencing techniques; you try assertive behaviour; you try being nice and working your network, and still you face an onslaught. At what point do you put aside the civil conventions of the office, and decide to stand and fight? This is a question which troubles everyone at some point, normally when the stakes are high.

Fortunately, there is a good guide for you. He is over 2,500 years old. Sun Tzu wrote *The Art of War*, and his advice of when to fight is as relevant to today's office as it was to China's warlords in the remote past.

Here are his three rules of warfare:

- Only fight when there is a prize worth fighting for.
- Only fight when you know you will win.
- Only fight when there is no other way of gaining your position.

don't fight unless you have to

In other words, don't fight unless you have to. Think back to the set-piece battles in your office over the last six months. The chances are that most of them failed at least one, and sometimes all three, of Sun Tzu's rules. And the chances are that they were pointless battles which did no one any good.

Let's look at each rule a little more closely.

Only fight when there is a prize worth fighting for

Don't worry about trivial contests. Minor slights and offences can be dealt with easily. Best to ignore the problem: don't waste energy and use up political capital on minor issues. If you can, concede gracefully, and make sure everyone knows that you have been the great team player who has conceded without arguing; even better, concede and ask for something in return.

But some contests are not trivial. Some prizes are well worth fighting for:

- fixing the right budget
- getting the right assignment
- finding the best team members
- gaining promotion, and possibly bonus
- enabling your project to complete on time.

These are high-value prizes. But follow Sun Tzu. Just because they are high value, it does not mean you should fight. The best battles are won without a shot being fired.

Only fight when you know you will win

Generals say that most battles are won or lost before the first shot is fired. What they mean is that one side will have the biggest and best army, the best equipment and the best position. The result is never in doubt.

The same rule applies in the office. If there is a fight to be won or lost, make sure you have all the right support lined up. That does not mean have all the best arguments: arguments are simply ammunition to support your position. Support means having the key decision makers and influencers on your side, while any opposition is isolated even if it is vocal.

If you are seen to fight and to lose, you will be damaged goods. You will look weak. On Wall Street and in poker there is a saying: 'if you don't know who the fall guy is, then you are'. If you don't know who is going to lose, you will lose. Make sure you line everything up for success. If your opposition is wise, they will normally see what is happening and quietly withdraw. If you are wise, you will then reach out to them and make sure they are not humiliated or offended: you need friends, not enemies.

If you have to fight, fight hard and make sure you win.

Only fight when there is no other way of gaining your position

As a rule, it is better to win a friend than win an argument. Leave the argument to another day, if you can. You can persuade a friend more easily than you can persuade an enemy. And an enemy may choose to harbour a grudge against you, drip poison about you onto the grapevine and make life unpleasant.

Dealing with rumour and innuendo

There are bitchy people and bitchy offices. There are two-faced people who smile to your face and trash you behind your back. It is not good being on the wrong end of rumour and gossip. The gossip can come in all shapes and sizes. Gossip passes judgement on you without either a trial or an examination of the evidence. Perceptions may be false, but the consequences of perceptions are real. So how do you deal with it?

Your challenge is that a script is being written about you: who you are and what you are like. You need to regain control of this script.

You have four broad lines of defence:

- **Reflect on what is being said.** If you think you are positive but others think you are negative, then ask yourself why these things are being said. You may say things in all innocence ('I was slightly disappointed by the widget proposal ...') which will then be taken as a massive attack and breach of confidence by the person who was responsible for the widget proposal. What you say and what is heard are completely different.

- **Play to your strengths.** Be true to yourself. You have to continue to role-model the sort of manager you want to be seen as. If you see yourself as the hard-charging, action-focused super-hero who puts out fires, that is fine. But don't be surprised if rumours start that you are not much of a team player. If you want to be seen as a great team player, make sure you act as a team player. But don't be surprised if the rumours start that you are not leading from the front. For every positive, there is a negative.

- **Act the part.** Being defensive, or counter-attacking, will not work. If you throw mud, you will land up with mud on yourself. Be positive, be confident, be proactive: be the role model for the organisation. It is very hard to make mud stick on someone who is a positive and confident role model: rumour only serves to make the rumour spreader look silly. And the best way to deny accusations of, say, being a poor team player is to demonstrate that you are a great team player and you enjoy it. Conversely, if you do not really care about teams, then make sure your other strengths overwhelm the problem of team playing. Play to your strengths.

- **Don't hide.** Normally, you will have a good idea about who is spreading the rumours. Make sure you bump into them in the canteen or elsewhere, and talk it through. You don't need to attack or confront. First, listen and find out what is going on. There may be an innocent explanation, or not. Either way, if

reflect; be true to
yourself; act the part;
don't hide

you handle the conversation positively the rumour spreader will normally be shamed into shutting up. And if they are simply playing politics, at least you know where you stand.

If the innuendo is becoming loud, talk to your boss. Repeat what you have been hearing and see if your boss agrees. Deal with it early, not late. If your boss agrees that there is some element of truth in the rumours, you can at least agree how to deal with it. The best way is to be very positive about it. If the innuendo says you are no good at the big picture (or detail), then this is your chance to profess huge enthusiasm for dealing with the big picture (or detail) when you get the chance. Or to say you want more experience in developing that capability. Turn the negative into a positive.

What do I do about consultants?

The consultants have landed. They are poking around, asking questions, doing interviews and conducting analyses. There is a widespread suspicion that they are going to re-engineer, out-source or offshore half the organisation; or that they are assessing staff to see who has a future. Fear, uncertainty and doubt follow. How should you react?

Most coaching situations are ambiguous and lead to 'On the one hand, but on the other hand …' sort of solutions. The arrival of consultants does not give rise to ambiguity. The solution to consultants is one-handed: there is no 'On the other hand …'.

Go out of your way to cooperate. Be helpful. Role-model the professional and proactive employee. You have nothing to lose, except your job. But you increase the risk of losing your job by being part of the awkward squad. The consultants will be reporting back to senior management, and it helps if they whisper good things about you in the right ears. If there is a cull, you want to be on the right side of the cull.

You may not like the consultants or the project they are working on. They may be overpaid, intrusive, demanding and dangerous. They may have a snotty attitude. All of that is irrelevant. Put aside your feelings. Focus on making them into your allies, not your enemies.

How do I tell someone they annoy me?

Small things can slowly turn a decent person into an axe-wielding maniac. It may be that a colleague plays music on headphones too loudly, or eats smelly food at the desk, or leaves everything a total mess, or always turns up late, or tells sarcastic jokes all the time, or just has annoying personal habits. You need to take action before you go and buy an axe and do something you might regret.

But you do not want to cause offence or create an enemy. And if someone annoys you because of their personal habits, that is your problem, not theirs. It is even possible that your perfectly reasonable habits reduce others to gibbering wrecks of frustration and anger. Whose problem is that?

Here is a simple two-step approach to try.

First, find a private place or moment when you are both in a good mood and you both happen to be together. Don't call a formal meeting about it; don't air dirty linen in public; don't deal with it when either of you is in a bad mood. Do it casually, positively and in private.

Second, have a very simple script which is in three parts:

- This is what you do (factual, no judgement).
- This is how it affects me (acknowledge this is your problem, not theirs).
- So could you help me? (by stopping, doing it elsewhere).

The script can, and should, be very short. For example: 'Your lunchtime curries look great … they're so good that the smell of them really distracts me, especially as it hangs around for a couple of hours … Could you help me by eating your curry elsewhere?'

The normal outcome is embarrassment followed by occasional efforts to eat the curry elsewhere. You will need to follow up. Make sure you thank them profusely when they help you by eating elsewhere. And if they eat curry at their desk again, have another word in private. Keep at it until the new habit is firmly in place.

If they get stroppy, leave it. It's your problem, unless you find the whole office is quietly being driven nuts by the same problem. Then you might escalate it.

If you are the boss, you have a bit more responsibility to take action. If a team member dresses like a tramp, doesn't wash properly or has annoying habits, you need to decide if those are just personal issues or if they affect the performance of your team and the individual. For instance, bad dress may be standard for an IT geek but unacceptable for a customer-facing role.

You can use roughly the same format as above, but more directly:

- This is what you do (facts, not interpretation).
- pause
- This is the impact it has (on me, on you, on the team, on performance).
- pause
- So what can we do about it? (problem solving, not telling).

Don't say 'you dress badly'. That invites an argument. Be specific: 'I notice you haven't worn a tie at all this week ….' This is factual. Then pause. Invite a reply. There may be a good reason, or you may be mistaken. Either way, agree the facts first.

Then indicate what you think the implications are. 'We need clients to see us as strong professionals: in our industry that means they expect to see us in suits and ties.' Then pause, and again invite a reply. If you need to have a discussion about client expectations and dress standards, this is a good time to have it.

> let them come up with a solution, rather than imposing your own

Finally, ask what can be done about it. Let them come up with a solution, rather than imposing your own. 'Wear a tie' may be obvious in this case. But the solution offered may be more creative: 'wear a tie when I'm going to a client meeting, but not in the office'. If that is an acceptable compromise, live with it.

Note

12 BBC radio broadcast, 1 October 1939.

Conclusion

As a coach, you will find yourself dealing with a huge variety of challenges. You will find yourself bouncing from one problem to the next. That is in the nature of the role. Over time, you will become better and better at helping yourself and your team deal with any problem, any challenge. You will become a better manager.

But to become the best manager you can, you need to go beyond dealing with problems. You need to build on what you are good at, and find the roles which play to your signature strengths. Manage your career journey well. The single strongest indicator of future success is to find people who enjoy what they do. I have yet to find a top professional who does not enjoy what they do, despite the long hours. Enjoyment is important, because only if you enjoy what you do will you put in the hours and go the extra mile year after year.

Your career journey is unique to you. But whatever your journey is, enjoy it.

Index